What to Do When
HOPE
is DEFERRED

"Hope is the word which God has written on the brow of every man" (Victor Hugo).

Tonya R. Williams

ISBN 978-1-64028-506-4 (paperback)
ISBN 978-1-64028-507-1 (digital)

Copyright © 2017 by Tonya R. Williams

All rights reserved. No part of this publication may be reproduced, distributed, or transmitted in any form or by any means, including photocopying, recording, or other electronic or mechanical methods without the prior written permission of the publisher. For permission requests, solicit the publisher via the address below.

Christian Faith Publishing, Inc.
832 Park Avenue
Meadville, PA 16335
www.christianfaithpublishing.com

Printed in the United States of America

CONTENTS

Acknowledgments 5

Chapter 1. Determine if Hope Is Truly Deferred 7

Chapter 2. Biblical Solutions to Consider 22

Chapter 3. Pray for Appropriate Application of the Scriptures.....36

Chapter 4. Trust Our Father in Heaven......................................48

Chapter 5. No Room for Doubt..61

Chapter 6. Stay Focused 73

Chapter 7. Obtain Godly Counsel 85

Chapter 8. Embrace the Revelations Gained 96

Chapter 9. Was the Suffering Worth It?....................................107

Chapter 10. Spread the Word...120

To my beautiful friend, Sara, may the God of the Bible I spoke of in this book, richly bless you and your family now, and forever!

Love,

Tonya R. Williams

ACKNOWLEDGMENTS

I do not believe that without divine intervention, this special moment in my life would be possible due to this thing that plagues me: human limitations.

I would like to give heartfelt appreciation and dedication of this book to The Most High God, to each of my deceased parents: Namon Irby, Dorothy, J. Thomas and my step-Father, Kimmie Thomas.

And I would like to make special acknowledgment to my husband, Vincent A. Williams, for always being "my rock" throughout the years.

Additionally, I would like to acknowledge my children, Anthony D. Bush, Eddie L. Bush, Derek Wood, and Vincent Williams Jr., for contributing to the countless growth experiences I discussed within the chapters.

I would like to acknowledge and say thank you to a special friend who really inspired me to write this book, namely, Rev. Dr. Lawrence C. Brown Sr. and his lovely bride, Christine Brown.

Writing my exposé of lessons learned, life experiences, and divine inspirations has held me mentally and emotionally captive for the last four years.

I graciously thank each one of you for being an intricate part of my life and for being the inspiration for this journey.

My prayer for each of you is that the God of the Bible will continue to richly bless and keep you.

CHAPTER 1

Determine if Hope Is Truly Deferred

According to the Bible, "*Hope deferred makes the heart sick, But desire fulfilled is a tree of life*" (Prov. 3:12, NASB).

For years, I have wondered why my heart was sick, and when I began to study the *scripture* written above, I gained immediate insight where to start.

Many years, I questioned myself with the following questions:

- Why my hope was deferred?
- Why did my dreams appear to be forfeited?
- Why had I not obtained set goals?

The questions listed above began a long internal quest to evaluate all the choices and decisions I had made from years past.

I began to think about realities that I did not want to think about.

And when I studied the aforementioned *scripture* for the very first time within the book of Proverbs, I knew there was serious soul-searching to do, and this was not easy, at all.

I was not comfortable with the thought that I was at fault for my "*deferred hope status*," and my heart was sick.

The thought I had actually made choices that had charted the course of my life in the opposite direction—this was actually devastating to even think about.

Throughout my quest for the hard truth, I had to ask myself more uncomfortable questions.

As you should do, I had to determine within myself, is my *hope really deferred*? If so, ask honestly, what decision or action did you or I make that caused hope to be deferred?

Or did *the Creator* divinely interrupt my or your world?

Have you prayed to *our Creator* for revelation?

Have you confessed sins?

Have you accepted responsibility?

Regardless of how you answered each question listed above, *our Father* still divinely orchestrated circumstances to have *His* perfect will be done.

I will say, *He* supernaturally works around the human element to use our circumstances to mold us to reflect *His* son, Jesus.

Let me clarify the above statement, those of us, who desire to reflect the image of our savior.

Are you a believer who said, "I want to be like Jesus" or "Father, mold me like Jesus"?

I can only answer for myself. Yes, I am one who prayed to be more like Jesus.

But what I did not realize at the time was *the Father* would use all my circumstances—good and bad—to remold me to be more like *His* son, Jesus.

Honestly dare to question your human psyche to answer the four aforementioned questions. This will be ambiguous and time consuming but necessary.

When I honestly searched myself, it was not long before I realized many of the personal issues I was dealing with came about due to thoughtless decisions and other choices I could not see at the time.

When you are only sixteen or seventeen years old, it is impossible to have the thinking process of a seasoned mature person. I am sure you can relate to this.

Again, it is not an easy thing to do—to self-evaluate ourselves. As a matter of fact, many of us avoid self-evaluating whenever possible.

Also, many of us take the easy way out by blaming others, and some even place the blame on people who had absolutely nothing to do with their situation(s).

If the last statement does not apply to you, I am sure you know someone who it does fit.

I felt the need to comment on the above because there are so many within the *body of Christ* who are not maturing, biblically or spiritually. Basically, there are many who need to be told the truth regarding accepting responsibility.

Beloved, embracing a destructive mind-set of blaming others will only lead to more heartache.

Plus, blaming others only prolongs the personal pain, not to mention the *deferred hope status*, and it extends or thwarts any possibility of healing.

Of course, if someone intentionally or unintentionally caused some of your pain, forgiveness is a good place to start. This will help you to heal from old wounds.

If you choose not to forgive, you will be playing a huge role in your own torment.

Please be mindful, when a believer does not accept responsibility for his or her actions or shifts blame, there are divine consequences, not to mention this will be potentially hurtful to your family and circle of friends, as they will be affected too.

So choose prayerfully and carefully how you proceed.

In determining why your "*hope is deferred,*" think about choices or actions you have made. Some choices could be from as early as your teenage years, or maybe there were bad choices while you were in your twenties, thirties, or forties or beyond. Other choices or actions can be more recent.

For instance, when I was just sixteen years of age, I decided to date a guy much older than myself. I did the unthinkable; I became pregnant and had my first child at seventeen years old. Imagine the circumstances surrounding this life-changing event.

Sadly, I thought I was doing the right thing by getting married so young. Looking back on it all, *totally clueless* does not describe my actual inexperience in those days.

I did not understand the weight and gravity of those decisions would have on my life until years later.

It was later on, while I was in my early twenties, that I understood the pain my mother must have endured. For a long time, I would not allow myself to think about it because I did not want to relive the terrible pain I caused her, not to mention myself.

As if I had not practically destroyed my chances of going to college, I made another bad decision shortly after becoming pregnant. I married at seventeen years old. Can you imagine? I made two bad choices in less than two months!

These two careless decisions charted the course of my life for many, many years. My life went in an entirely different direction, to say the least.

Basically, the main key to obtaining an understanding in relation to your "*hope deferred status*" is to accept responsibility.

There is no other way.

Please ignore our society's loud cries, which say without fail that in many ways, you do not have to accept responsibility.

I realize accepting responsibility or being accountable for one's actions is no longer a popular mind-set to possess within the twenty-first century.

Actually, accepting responsibility for one's actions has become a relative action, if not politically correct. People choose the path of least resistance or whatever feels good to them, thus avoiding responsibility.

Note, embracing this mind-set will lead to more destructive choices that will have a long-term effect on your life and others in your circle.

However, accepting responsibility is necessary in order to engage *our Creator* for help.

Maybe you did nothing. If this is true, congratulations, but remember, there must be honest and real soul-searching in your quest. Also, please remember, according to the *Scriptures, we are not without sin.*

> "*If we say that we have no sin, we deceive ourselves, and the truth is not in us*" (1 John 1:8, KJV).

WHAT TO DO WHEN HOPE IS DEFERRED

> *"If we say that we have not sinned, we make him a liar, and his word is not in us"* (1 John 1:10, KJV).

These are strong words from the Bible *scriptures* ordained by *our Creator*.

As you can, see it is absolutely critical for you to be truthful to yourself and God. You see, *the Father* already knows everything. *He* is waiting for you to humble yourself, confess your sins, and seek forgiveness.

There is a light at the end of the tunnel, which is *our Father's* forgiveness.

> *"If we confess our sins, he is faithful and just to forgive us our sins, and to cleanse us from all unrighteousness"* (1 John 1:9 KJV).

Moreover, in life, when *"hope is deferred"* or *"something we desired is not fulfilled,"* sometimes this is contributed by a decision or choice we made. This is not always the case, but most of the time, it is.

It is very hard for one to admit to themselves that they have played a key role in their *hope being deferred*. Simply stated, I had to come to terms with it personally, and it was not easy.

Perhaps someone caused your altered state directly or indirectly. Either way, the choices you made after the fact could have contributed to your *deferred hope status*.

As a matter of fact, I attempted on several occasions to avoid self-evaluation, but avoiding admitting my failures did not work. Nor was life working for me doing things my way. Sometimes, I cannot believe *He* spared my life while I was in my idiotic stance.

The more I studied the *Scriptures*, the more I became convicted of current and past sins.

Please know that current and past sins (or past sinful choices) will contribute to your *"hope deferred status."* Do not be fooled. Sin has a way of catching up with us.

Our Father in heaven will not ignore sin—past or present. There must be a contrite confession of your sins.

Actually, it is better for us to examine or self-evaluate than cause *our Father* to divinely intervene.

> *"Examine yourselves, whether ye be in the faith; prove your own selves. Know ye not your own selves, how that Jesus Christ is in you, except ye be reprobates"* (2 Cor. 13:5–6, KJV).

Basically, the above *scripture* challenges a professing Christian to test themselves, so all professing the Christian faith must examine themselves to determine if they are truly born again.

The *scriptures* above are a charge from God to always self-evaluate regarding our spiritual condition. The consequences for a believer not examining themselves could be dire.

You see, *the Father* has "*no respect of persons.*" This applies to us all.

> "*For there is no respect of persons with God*" (Rom. 2:11, KJV).

The Father is not concerned if you are rich or poor, educated or uneducated, with degrees around the wall, or if you are African American, Caucasian, Asian, or whether you live in Tatum, Texas, or if your residence is in Anchorage, Alaska.

All who consider themselves born again through Jesus Christ must adhere to *His* word. There are no exceptions.

This is not an effort to frighten anyone, but it is to benefit all who adhere.

Unfortunately, some believers have chosen to ignore or to even forfeit self-evaluation. It is hard to imagine any believer embracing an attitude of this nature.

However, within the *body of Christ*, there are various levels of spiritual maturity with believers, so there will be some who gravitate to an easier way out. Unfortunately, the easy way out is not what some believe it to be, but all must give an accounting later.

Sometimes, less mature believers take the easier way out or the less traveled path to hold tight to their stance. Even if their position is wrong, unbeknownst to them or in their denial, there will be consequences. This chapter is to encourage less biblically mature believers to seek wise counsel.

Please be mindful, wise counsel can come from studying the Word of God, the *Holy Spirit* (the third person of the Trinity) ministering to your spiritual man or woman, or a biblically-aligned counselor.

There are three persons of the Trinity, namely, *the Father* (God), the Son (*Jesus*), and the *Holy Spirit*.

Jesus instructed the disciples, *"Go therefore and make disciples of all the nations, baptizing them in the name of the Father and the Son and the Holy Spirit"* (Matt. 28:19, NASB).

The Bible verses within the book of Proverbs provide a wealth of biblical teachings regarding seeking wise counseling. King Solomon was the son of David within the Bible, and Solomon was the wisest man to have ever lived. He was a prolific writer who wrote the Proverbs, Psalms, and the Song of Solomon books within the Bible.

In Proverbs 1, Solomon explains in depth why he wrote this extraordinary book:

> *"To know wisdom and instruction; to perceive the words of understanding"* (Prov. 1:2, KJV).

> *"To receive the instruction of wisdom, justice, and judgment, and equity"* (Prov. 1:3, KJV).

Solomon desired his son to be wise in all decisions; therefore, he provided sound biblical instructions to him within the book of Proverbs.

"A wise man will hear, and will increase learning; and a man of understanding shall attain unto wise counsels" (Prov. 1:5, KJV).

"The fear of the Lord is the beginning of knowledge; fools despise wisdom and instruction" (Prov. 1:7, KJV).

"Listen to my instruction and be wise; do not ignore it. Blessed is the man who listens to me, watching daily at my doors, waiting at my doorway. For whoever finds me finds life and receives favor from the Lord" (Prov. 8:32–35, NIV).

It would greatly benefit us all, no matter where you are with your walk in Christ, to always study the Bible. I admit, I am partial to the book of Proverbs.

Note that all the books of the Bible were written for correction and reproof, to build a low tolerance of sin within our lives. Actually, the book of Proverbs will be a great antidote to sinful choices for any believer who desires to grow spiritually.

Of course, on the other side of the fence, an ungodly attitude will bring about another set of issues. The previous statement only applies to anyone who thinks in this destructive capacity.

Some have chosen to travel down this destructive road, to their own hurt and destruction of their lives. Many times over, others are affected too.

The thing about ignoring sin is that it hurts the individual who choose this route, but sin also hurts the people in their lives too. Choose carefully your course of action. In my own life, I have observed over the years the long-term fallout from my sinful choices.

To clarify, each one of my sons, to this day, struggle with submitting "their wills" to *our Creator*. All my boys have a rebellious spirit.

Remember, the ole folks used to say, "You will see yourself [sin] again in your kids, down the road." And I still see their ongoing sinful choices and the effects of it.

I had it wrong; the ole folks knew exactly what they were talking about. Although when the ole folks from back home was telling me this, I ignorantly thought they did not know what they were talking about.

I have found from a biblical standpoint that there is the law of sowing and reaping.

> *"Be not deceived; God is not mocked: for whatsoever a man soweth, that shall he also reap" (Gal. 6:7, KJV).*

For the sake of simplicity, if you are making ungodly choices, you will reap ungodly rewards. If you are making godly or biblical choices, you will reap godly rewards.

On another front, when *"hope is divinely deferred,"* there are other spiritual dynamics occurring in the background. Spiritual dynamics related to hope deferred will be addressed in the following chapter.

How many of us will take time to self-evaluate this very important point, truthfully?

Self-evaluating one's actions or choices immediately can be liberating. In addition, self-evaluation is a calming psychological antidote when prayer is included.

When we are in prayer confessing our sins, *He* will reveal our bad choices or actions. I will say, such actions require a humble, and a submitted heart.

According to the *Scriptures, He* will forgive us of all unrighteousness.

Is asking *our Father's* forgiveness worth it? Yes, by all means, asking for *His* forgiveness is worth it—for many reasons. If you desire a clear conscious and for your guilt to be erased, then asking for forgiveness is necessary.

I will step out and suggest praying and crying out to *the Father*, like David did in the *Scriptures*. This will get your sin out in the open. Trust me, *the Father* already knows. *He's* just waiting for you to humble yourself before *Him*. I cried out!

The Psalms are filled with an abundance of prayers and songs and with David crying out to God for forgiveness and divine assistance. These are examples for us all.

> *"But thou, O LORD, art a shield for me; my glory, and the lifter up of mine head" (Ps. 3:3, KJV).*

> *"I cried unto the LORD with my voice, and he heard me out of his holy hill. Selah" Ps. 3:4, KJV).*

> *"I laid me down and slept; I awaked; for the LORD sustained me" (Ps. 3:5).*

As we humble ourselves, *He* is able to divinely intervene on our behalf. The keyword in the last sentence is *humble*.

Unfortunately, many believers totally ignore this. *Our Father* only gives grace to the humble.

> *"Surely he scorneth the scorners: but he giveth grace unto the lowly" (Prov. 3:34, KJV)*

The Bible is not like a secular book, where one can pick and choose what they like and discard what they do not like. Nor is the Bible a smorgasbord where people can pick and choose what feels good to them or anything of the kind. The *scriptures* are all God-breathed and are for our reproof and correction.

> *"All scripture is given by inspiration of God, and is profitable for doctrine, for reproof, for correction, for instruction in righteousness" (2 Tim. 2:16, KJV).*

According to the *Scriptures*, "But he giveth more grace. Wherefore he saith, God resisteth the proud, but giveth grace unto the humble" (James 4:6, KJV).

Those who choose to humble themselves will be blessed because *His* Word does not return back to *Him* void. And it is a choice.

> *"So shall my word be that goeth forth out of my mouth: it shall not return unto me void, but it shall accomplish that which I please, and it shall prosper in the thing whereto I sent it"* (Isa. 55:11, KJV)

Remember, blessings may not be anything physical you can touch. As a matter of fact, *our Father* does not do *quid pro quo* like the world does. For example, "Do something for me, and I will do something for you."

The Father owes us nothing; however, by *His* unmerited grace, *He* has given us eternal life, but do we really deserve it? *He* is our Creator, and we are *His* creations. *He* created us to serve and worship *Him*.

Unfortunately, in many twenty-first century congregations, this is not being taught.

The secular world rewards people for this or that; however, *our Father* does not operate in this fashion.

I thought this was an important point to make. I have observed over the years this sort of mentality in some believers.

The above behavior is not indicative of every believer, but there are some within the *body of Christ* who recklessly adopt this mind-set.

> *"As for you, if you will walk before Me as your father David walked, in integrity of heart and uprightness, doing according to all that I have commanded you and will keep My statutes and My ordinances"* (2 Sam. 9:4, NASB).

You see, as a believer grows in grace, knowledge, and wisdom in God's Word with application in their daily lives, there is a genuine spiritual metamorphous that occurs.

A believer residing in the above state is constantly growing, confessing their sins constantly, submitting their will, and living in obedience to *His* will.

There are countless spiritual blessings to a submitted believer who lives in obedience to *His* will. As an obedient spirit-growing believer lives, he or she yields to the "fruit of the spirit," which are blessings from *our Creator*.

> *"But the fruit of the Spirit is love, joy, peace, long-suffering, gentleness, goodness, faith"* (Gal. 5:22, KJV).

Sure, these folks fall off the wagon too because remember, as I said earlier, no one is without sin.

More importantly, a submitted believer understands and embraces *our Father's* ways and will oppose their own ways. Is this you?

As believers, we all should be staying in *His* Word daily, in addition to daily constant application for real growth.

The *Scriptures* say, *"Study to shew thyself approved unto God, a workman that needeth not to be ashamed, rightly dividing the word of truth"* (2 Tim. 2:15, KJV).

The studying and daily application of God's Word will cause an immature believer to grow in grace wonderfully.

Also, a mature believer is an asset to the *body of Christ* or believers for service. Did anyone ever tell you that born-again believers are "servants"? This is our reasonable service—to serve others and the body of Christ.

> *"I beseech you therefore, brethren, by the mercies of God, that ye present your bodies a living sacrifice, holy, acceptable unto God, which is your reasonable service"* (Rom. 12:1, KJV).

Now remember, all born-again believers still struggle with sin on a daily basis, if not on an hourly basis or minute by minute. Many believers understand the importance of studying the Word daily. Actually, studying the Bible and applying God's commandments serves as a believer's antidote to their sinful natures. This is the only way I can be controlled, and I am happy I understand this critical point in my walk. Men and women alike have a natural inclination to sin and to like it. Have you heard the old saying, "This book will keep you from sin, but sin will keep you from this book"?

Of course, this is not a biblical saying, but the quote hits at the heart of what every believer must deal with—sin.

Within our progressive twenty-first century society, one can tie all the ills our society is facing to sin. However, mainstream media will never broadcast the issues of man in direct correlation to his ongoing sinful nature, which continues to dominate.

Jesus was tempted in the wilderness by Satan, and the *scriptures* Jesus quoted to Satan ring true for every born-again believer today.

Please read below:

> *"Then Jesus was led up by the Spirit into the wilderness to be tempted by the devil. And after fasting forty days and forty nights, he was hungry. And the tempter came and said to him, 'If you are the Son of God, command these stones to become loaves of bread.' But he answered, 'It is written, Man shall not live by bread alone, but by every word that comes from the mouth of God'"* (Matt. 4:1–4).

Sadly, the masses still believe it is okay to live without acceptance of *our Creator's* governance and believe *everything will be all right*. It is simply not true, and as a matter of fact, this is an outright lie, according to the *Scriptures*. One can study history before Christ (BC) and after Christ (AD) to see well-documented stories of how nation after nation fell without *the Father's* governance.

Men desired men to be kings to rule over them instead of *our Creator*. Can you see the similarity compared to American culture today?

> *"When Samuel grew old, he appointed his sons as Israel's leaders, The name of his firstborn was Joel and the name of his second was Abijah, and they*

served at Beersheba. But his sons did not follow his ways. They turned aside after dishonest gain and accepted bribes and perverted justice. So all the elders of Israel gathered together and came to Samuel at Ramah. They said to him, "You are old, and your sons do not follow your ways; now appoint a king to lead us, such as all the other nations have" (1 Sam. 8:1–5, KJV).

This mind-set in any man is problematic for several reasons. I will address a few reasons to enlighten all who reject this prideful and arrogant stance. First, without *our Creator's* divine protection from ourselves, *"all we like sheep have gone astray; we have turned everyone to his own way; and the LORD hath laid on him the iniquity of us all"* (Isa. 53:6, KJV).

Simply stated, since we are mere humans with an abundance of limitations, which includes but is not limited to spiritual shortfalls and lack of knowledge, we should not be going our own way! The Old and New Testament prove over and over again that we cannot survive without *Him*.

Second, we make numerous bad choices again and again, which will all but ensure that our *hope is deferred*.

When the Israelites rejected God's (our Creator's) protection, they were taken into captivity continuously by godless nations. Do you prefer to be taken captive by your sinful choices? Additionally, Satan will enjoy picnicking at your camp. Who needs this nightmare?

Third, without His divine protection and direction, the enemy will have full rule over your life. You see, we need *our Creator* to guide our every step by prayer with supplication and complete application. It is all or nothing!

I presented only a few reasons to share with you the potential fallout from not having *His* divine protection. There are countless more reasons within the *Scripture* pages.

By seriously considering the above biblical commentary, you will avoid unnecessary grief for yourself and your circle, not to mention begin a long overdue healing process from past decisions or choices that caused *hope to be deferred.*

The lessons you learn will be instrumental in assisting others to overcome their "*hope deferred*" status for years to come.

And those helped will influence the next generations to come and so on.

CHAPTER 2

Biblical Solutions to Consider

"Cast your cares on the LORD and he will sustain you; he will never let the righteous fall" (Ps. 55:22, KJV).

As a submitted born-again believer within the *body of Christ*, there are several biblically based options to consider.

Earlier, I alluded to considering biblical solutions in the first chapter, which would be instrumental during your time of soul-searching.

At the onset of soul-searching, many believers have difficulty overcoming or even recognizing hindrances. I am referring to *His* least desired characteristics many of us possess, such as pride and arrogance.

Simply explained, *"These six things the LORD hates, Yes, seven are an abomination to Him: A proud look, A lying tongue, Hands that shed innocent blood, A heart that devises wicked plans, Feet that are swift in running to evil, A false witness who speaks lies, And one who sows discord among brethren"* (Prov. 6:16–19, KJV).

For the sake of clarification, I am referring to "a proud look." This clearly points to our natural sinful nature, to exude pride and arrogance when we are confronted with potential self-evaluation.

Many of us do not want to face the possibility that we may have made a choice that caused our *"hope to be deferred."* This attitude is rooted totally in arrogance and pride. It is easier and more comfortable to avoid accepting responsibility for one's actions.

I have known family members who were so prideful and arrogant to the point that they destroyed their families, and certain family members did not give it a second thought, all for the sake of them "being right."

However, when one rejects the fact that he or she has made bad choices that has caused their spiritual dilemma, "*hope is further deferred.*" It is impossible for the *God of the Bible* to render aid through *His* Word and prayer if one will not humble themselves.

Sadly, this is the mind-set of countless believers. It is hard to believe this happens, but yet it is true.

That said, many have forfeited God's best for themselves simply due to their stiff-necked stance. You see, *He* does not care about one's prideful or arrogant positions, *He* only cares about *His* glory and for *His* will to be done.

Do you remember the *scripture* in Matthew 6:10?

> "*Thy kingdom come. Thy will be done in earth, as it is in heaven*" *(Matt. 6:10, KJV).*

The Father is clear in *His* Word that "*His* will be done," not ours!

If you choose to go against *His* will for your life by not confessing sins or by embracing a prideful mind-sets, be ready for chaos because chaos is what your life will be until you do surrender all authority and your will to *Him*. I am speaking from the standpoint of experience.

Remember in the first chapter, we discussed the Israelites' disobedience to God and what it led to. As a brief reminder, the Israelites (or Hebrew children) were taken away in captivity over and over again due to disobedience and their stiff-necked stances on many things all throughout the book of the Kings and Chronicles.

The Israelites did not want *the Father* to be their God. They wanted a king to rule over them like their ungodly neighbors in 1 Samuel 8.

The fallout from the Israelites rejecting *His* rule was tremendous.

Fast-forwarding to the twenty-first century, if a man or a woman rejects God's sovereignty over them, the results can and will be costly.

You can lose the Lord's absolute best for your life. Many have taken this route.

Of course, there is the other side of the camp that chose to accept responsibility for their choices or actions. Thus, these folks seek biblically based guidance, prayer, and godly counseling.

These true believers study the Bible constantly, confess sins, pray, attend church regularly, and have submitted wills.

Please permit me to elaborate, even if a believer does all the right biblical things, it does not mean their life will be a cakewalk. Many times over, these folks are tested too, with temptations, tribulations, hardships, bad health, and other human ills.

Because these sold-out believers are human too, and I liken their suffering to that of Job. Please study the Book of Job at your leisure.

Basically, there are two sides: those who accept responsibility for their choices and those who do not. This simple analogy begs the question, which side of the camp are you on?

Note, there is no in between. Choose.

Do you as a believer desire to evolve into a mature Christian? Or is it your desire to remain in self-denial regarding your circumstances? The latter choice brings chaos, confusion, and more sinful choices as you go forward.

This book was written with you in mind as a simple, no-nonsense, and biblically aligned guide to provoke real biblical thought processes for real change.

Additionally, within the following pages, I will layout biblical solutions I implemented within my universe. These biblical solutions helped to console and heal my heart during very difficult years.

When I made the decision many years ago to seek *His* best for my life, everything changed in my world—for the better.

Well, I had met a pastor who was actually my property maintenance man in an apartment complex my kids and I resided at during the mid-1980s. Brother Smith invited me, my sister, and our children to attend his church. So we did.

After attending church there for a few months, I began to receive unction or prompting to learn more about God's Word. I know now this was the *Holy Spirit*, but of course, during that time, I did not have a clue.

So I began attending Bible study every Wednesday evening at the local church I was attending at that time in the mid-1980s.

The church I attended was Baptist, and it was located in Dallas, Texas. At first, attending Bible study with the aging senior pastor was daunting.

The elder pastor would go into long explanations about *Scripture* lessons, which further added to my confusion. In addition, the pastor provided very detailed biblically based manuals to assist me with the class and studying.

I settled in to learn because honestly I knew the pastor knew more than I did.

In the pastor's honest attempt to keep his teaching method simple, his method of teaching became a learning hindrance for me.

There came a point when I realized there was so much more to learn about the *Scriptures* than what I was learning under my well-intentioned pastor.

I began to pray to *the Father* for help in obtaining an understanding regarding *His* Word. I needed an understanding, which I lacked.

> *"Wisdom is the principal thing; Therefore get wisdom. And in all your getting, get understanding"* (Prov. 4:7, KJV).

I studied over the *scripture* that said, "*But the Comforter, who is the Holy Spirit, whom the Father will send in my name, he shall teach you all things, and bring all things to your remembrance, whatsoever I have said unto you*" (John 14:26, KJV).

> *"Nevertheless I tell you the truth; It is expedient for you that I go away: for if I go not away, the*

> *Comforter will not come unto you; but if I depart, I will send him unto you"* (John 16:7, KJV).

> *"But when the Comforter is come, whom I will send unto you from the Father, even the Spirit of truth, which proceedeth from the Father, he shall testify of me"* (John 15:26, KJV).

> *"And ye also shall bear witness, because ye have been with me from the beginning"* (John 15:27, KJV).

After studying the above *scriptures*, I believed it! And I began to pray for the *Holy Spirit* to teach God's Word to me. This was a critical turning point for me when it came to Bible studying. My life changed forever!

Beloved, be encouraged, because *He* will do the same for you.

I continued to attend formal Bible study, but the above *scriptures* empowered my thought processes, which transcended beyond a human teaching me.

Although I have continued to be taught by gifted Bible teachers, I depend totally on the *Holy Spirit* to interpret the *Scriptures*.

I hope you can see the importance of attending Bible study because had I not attended Bible study, I would have not developed a *hunger and thirst* for *His* Word.

> *"Who desires all men to be saved and to come to the knowledge of the truth"* (1 Tim. 2:4, KJV)

You see, *our Father* divinely orchestrated *His* will for me through this elderly pastor.

By the way, Reverend P loved the Lord, and *our Father* used him, greatly.

The more I studied, the more I wanted to study. I could not get enough of studying *His* Word and coming to the knowledge of the whole truth.

In those days, I was a package delivery driver for a major package delivery company in Mesquite, Texas. I worked long hours daily.

My day would begin at 5:30 a.m. in the morning.

By this time, I had married again, so my husband and I had a total of four boys. The boys were very young, so I cooked breakfast for them before heading off to work every morning.

Moreover, I could not control my desire to study the Bible, so I would study into the early morning hours as much as possible. I could not wait for my twelve-hour workdays to end so I could race home to study the Bible.

With studying the Bible, there was conviction of past and present sins. You see, if you are studying the *Scriptures* with intent—I mean with intent to change—there will be transformation of how you think and feel about your sin.

Plus, there is something I never expected to occur in those days—I began to see the people and the world from *our Father's* point of view. I began to have experience a rash of emotions that kept me weeping all the time. I despised the fallout of what my sin had caused.

I began to understand exactly why my family and the rest of the world was in such chaos. One word described it all—*sin*. We all had embraced sin as if it was good for us.

I truly began to see my own self-validated hypocrisy, which ruled my life. I began to see that according to the *Scriptures*, I was not much more than a filthy rag.

> *"But we are all as an unclean thing, and all our righteousnesses are as filthy rags; and we all do fade as a leaf; and our iniquities, like the wind, have taken us away" (Isa. 64:6, KJV).*

I began to see, all of us had left our *"first love"*—God, the Father.

> *"Nevertheless I have somewhat against thee, because thou hast left thy first love" (Rev. 2:4, KJV).*

I began to see and understand that I was not righteous, nor was I a good person.

In effort to share with you *His* words, which were instrumental in my transformation process, please read below:

> "God forbid: yea, let God be true, but every man a liar; as it is written, That thou mightest be justified in thy sayings, and mightest overcome when thou art judged.
>
> "But if our unrighteousness commend the righteousness of God, what shall we say? Is God unrighteous who taketh vengeance? (I speak as a man)
>
> "God forbid: for then how shall God judge the world? For if the truth of God hath more abounded through my lie unto his glory; why yet am I also judged as a sinner? And not rather, (as we be slanderously reported, and as some affirm that we say,) Let us do evil, that good may come? whose damnation is just.
>
> "What then? are we better than they? No, in no wise: for we have before proved both Jews and Gentiles, that they are all under sin;
>
> "As it is written, There is none righteous, no, not one:
>
> "There is none that understandeth, there is none that seeketh after God.
>
> "They are all gone out of the way, they are together become unprofitable; there is none that doeth good, no, not one.
>
> "Their throat is an open sepulchre; with their tongues they have used deceit; the poison of asps is under their lips:
>
> "Whose mouth is full of cursing and bitterness:
>
> "Their feet are swift to shed blood:
>
> "Destruction and misery are in their ways:
>
> "And the way of peace have they not known:

> *"There is no fear of God before their eyes. Now we know that what things soever the law saith, it saith to them who are under the law: that every mouth may be stopped, and all the world may become guilty before God.*
>
> *"Therefore by the deeds of the law there shall no flesh be justified in his sight: for by the law is the knowledge of sin.*
>
> *"But now the righteousness of God without the law is manifested, being witnessed by the law and the prophets;*
>
> *"Even the righteousness of God which is by faith of Jesus Christ unto all and upon all them that believe: for there is no difference: For all have sinned, and come short of the glory of God"* (Rom. 3:4–23, KJV).

Please know that the entire Bible transformed me into *His* likeness, and I am still transforming. *He* will use the Scriptures to transform you too.

Just in case you are not aware, *our Father* cannot and will not look upon sin.

> *"[Thou art] of purer eyes than to behold evil, and canst not look on iniquity: wherefore lookest thou upon them that deal treacherously, [and] holdest thy tongue when the wicked devoureth [the man that is] more righteous than he"* (Hab. 1:13, KJV).

Sin alienates us from *our Father.*

Beloved, this is why it is absolutely critical and a necessity for you to acknowledge and confess your sins daily, if not hourly.

Also, do not become caught up with those who know something to be wrong and still do it. You will not be guiltless.

> *"Therefore to him that knoweth to do good, and doeth it not, to him it is sin"* (James 4:17, KJV).

Our Father has strong warnings regarding hypocrisy and a sinful lifestyle under the delusion that it is Christianity.

Many within the household of faith have chosen this route, to their own destruction. Some who choose this path have been headlines on mainstream media outlets.

Basically, for a believer who has embraced hypocrisy as their method of self-validation, their hopes is God will embrace their version of truth.

This could not be further from reality. It is almost inconceivable to think that there are some within the *body of Christ* who take this mind-boggling stance.

Moreover, the *Scriptures* offer strong warnings to those who choose this route.

Study and practice the following biblical instructions:

> *"Beware of practicing your righteousness before other people in order to be seen by them, for then you will have no reward from your Father who is in heaven"* (Matt. 6:1, KJV).

> *"You hypocrite, first take the log out of your own eye, and then you will see clearly to take the speck out of your brother's eye"* (Matt. 7:5 KJV).

> *"You hypocrites! Well did Isaiah prophesy of you, when he said: 'This people honors me with their lips, but their heart is far from me; in vain do they worship me, teaching as doctrines the commandments of men"* (Matt. 15:7–9 KJV).

> *"Do you suppose, O man—you who judge those who practice such things and yet do them yourself—*

that you will escape the judgment of God" (Rom. 2:3, KJV).

You see, there is not one of us who is without fault, and *He* is not impressed with those who choose hypocrisy as a way of life. *His* stern warnings about practicing sin will yield *"the ultimate judgment."* Also, the warnings and penalties become more grievous and definite within the book of Revelations.

This is why *our Father* sent *His* only begotten son, Jesus, as a proxy or replacement for our sin.

> *"For God so loved the world, that he gave his only begotten Son, that whosoever believeth in him should not perish, but have everlasting life" (John 3:16, KJV).*

It is not *His* will that we perish from choosing to embrace our sin. *Our Father* made a way out for each of us.

Going forward through the direction and inspiration of the *Holy Spirit*, you will begin to despise your sin and the sin of others, period. This is how *our Father in heaven* feels about sin.

Additionally, as you study and apply the *Scriptures*, you will begin to see the destruction and ravages of the effects of sin clearly.

When the transformation began, through prayer, I asked *the Father* to reveal *all* my sin to me.

I can say this now, I was not emotionally prepared to deal with all my past sins *He* revealed. *His* Word, *His* mercy and prayers were my only saving grace.

This was a blessed time, and it was torment. It was extremely difficult to see my reflection shining back at me in the mirror (the Bible).

It was during this stage in my life, I was able to get a grip on past choices and decisions that had ravaged my world.

I thank *the Father* for *His* grace and restorative power because *He* has mercifully restored in my life what the locusts had eaten up.

> *"Then I will make up to you for the years That the swarming locust has eaten, The creeping locust, the stripping locust and the gnawing locust, My great army which I sent among you" (Joel 2:25, NASB).*

I am a living witness. *He* will reestablish *His* perfect will in your life. Believe it or not, the occurrence of the last aforementioned sentence is all up to you.

Why did I say that, you ask?

When you make the decision to humble yourself before the *King of kings* and *Lord of lords, He* can and will help you.

First, you must humble yourself and tell him all about your sin of arrogance, pride, hypocrisy, and so on. You see, according to *His* Word, *our Father* only gives grace to the humble.

Plus, *our Father* deals with a broken and contrite heart. Your broken spirit is precious in *His* sight. When you have surrendered, this signals *Him* you have humbled yourself.

> *"The sacrifices of God are a broken spirit: a broken and a contrite heart, O God thou wilt not despise" (Ps 51:17, KJV).*

On another front, the *scriptures* are clear regarding the other side of the camp for those who hold tightly to their pride and arrogant stance.

> *"The fear of the LORD is to hate evil: pride, and arrogancy, and the evil way, and the forward mouth, do I hate" (Prov. 8:18, KJV).*

> *"Pride goeth before destruction, and an haughty spirit before a fall" (Prov. 16:18 KJV).*

> *"Better it is to be of an humble spirit with the lowly, than to divide the spoil with the proud" (Prov. 16:19, KJV).*

The definition of *haughty* is "arrogant," as defined by *Dictionary.com*.

> *"He mocks proud mockers but gives grace to the humble" (Prov. 3:34, NIV).*

> *"But he giveth more grace. Wherefore he saith, God resisteth the proud, but giveth grace unto the humble" (James 4:6, KJV).*

Second, you must seek *His* divine forgiveness.

The beauty of asking for forgiveness from *our Father* is *He* will forgive us for all unrighteousness.

> *"If we confess our sins, he is faithful and just to forgive us our sins, and to cleanse us from all unrighteousness" (1 John 1:9, KJV).*

So you can see the trouble, many within the *body of Christ* get themselves into when disregarding *His* stern and clear warnings. All the above destructive attributes will only lead to your prayers not being answered and pretty much a miserable existence.

Third, there is no one who is above confession of their sins—I reiterate, no one. Every believer must go through this process in order to have real fellowship with *the Father*. As I previously addressed, *He* does not deal in any sin, so much so that *He* was willing to send *His* only begotten son to die in our place as propitiation for our sins.

> *"For God so loved the world, that he gave his only begotten Son, that whosoever believeth in him should not perish, but have everlasting life" (John 3:16, KJV).*

If you are in denial regarding your sinful nature and propensity to sin, this is the time to lay it down at *His* feet. You see, tomorrow is not promised to any of us. As a matter of fact, from the day each one of us was born, we have been "on the clock." The clock is ticking away on our lives that we think belong to us. This is simply not true because those of us born again were bought with a high price.

> *"For you have been bought with a price: therefore glorify God in your body" (1 Cor. 6:20, KJV).*

Plus, the book of James said our lives are but a vapor.

> *"Yet you do not know what your life will be like tomorrow. You are just a vapor that appears for a little while and then vanishes away" (James 4:14, KJV).*

These *scriptures* listed above confirmed in my heart that I do not have time to "play church" or to ignore *the Father's* words. I certainly hope this is your take as well.

How often do many forfeit *His* truth for a lie? I make this statement because if you accept any other version of truth apart from the Bible, it is a lie.

For many within the *body of Christ* have deceived themselves into believing falsehood is the truth.

Thus, some believers are living in daily chaos, denial, and confusion because they will not surrender to *His* truth.

I have observed over the years people living their lives based on their own version of what truth is, and these folks profess to be born-again Christians. Many people have a natural inclination to do things their way. I remember a song sung by Frank Sinatra titled "I Did It My Way," recorded in 1969. Unfortunately, many within the *body of Christ* believe they can do things *their way* and believe there will not be divine consequences. This mind-set could not be further from the truth. Actually, it is quite the opposite for those who confess to be believers. There will be undeniable divine chastening from *our Father in Heaven*. There are always divine consequences for sin.

> *"For whom the Lord loveth he chasteneth, and scourgeth every son whom he receiveth" (Heb. 12:6, KJV).*

I am hopeful this chapter has given you clear-cut biblical solutions to correct the unpleasant direction your life maybe going. Beloved, you will be greatly blessed by applying these ageless biblical principles to your life. Also, your loved ones, friends, and the people you encounter in the *body of Christ* will truly be the benefactors of your changed heart and mind. Plus, you will no longer have to live under the curse of sin, which are, but not limited to, disappointment, discouragement, despair, doubt, disbelief, double-mindedness, delay, dishonesty, deceit, discord, defame, defilement, discontent, disobedience, and debt.

> *"Lest Satan should get an advantage of us: for we are not ignorant of his devices" (2 Cor. 2:11, KJV).*

You will be free from Satan's devices. And it is then you will be able discover what *His* purpose for your life is through prayer and supplication.

I am so glad my worst days no longer define me.

The chains of sin and bondage will be broken for you too!

CHAPTER 3

Pray for Appropriate Application of the Scriptures

"Praying at all times in the Spirit, with all prayer and supplication. To that end keep alert with all perseverance, making supplication for all the saints" (Eph. 6:18, KJV).

As a born-again believer, it is crucial for your spiritual growth to apply the *Scriptures* appropriately. One must live a life of obedience according to the *Scriptures*, to *our Father's* will for their lives. By properly applying the *Scriptures* to the issue of *"your deferred hope,"* He will cause you to develop hope.

Simply said, *our Father* honors our complete obedience, regardless of our life issues. Whether we feel wronged or slighted, it is incumbent upon us to yield to *His* Word.

Have you read the *scripture* 1 Samuel 5:18?

"And Samuel said, 'Has the Lord as great delight in burnt offerings and sacrifices, as in obeying the voice of the Lord? Behold, to obey is better than sacrifice, and to listen than the fat of rams.'"

According to 1 Thessalonians 5:17 (NASB), we are to *"pray without ceasing."*

I realize that sometimes life happens to us, and it does not always afford us the time or place for ongoing prayer. I submit to you, there are *no formal* places to have prayer.

One can have prayer anywhere, anytime. For instance, early in the morning before the world attacks you is a perfect time.

Actually, on the way to work or during work, pray for a few minutes. The main thing to remember, just pray all throughout each day.

Another thing to note, from the onset of your prayer, confess your sins.

> *"If we confess our sins, he is faithful and righteous to forgive us our sins, and to cleanse us from all unrighteousness" (1 John 1:9, KJV).*

"No one can go before *Our Creator,* as if he or she is without sin. This will only cause more problems for you. *If we say that we have not sinned, we make Him a liar and His word is not in us" (1 John 1:10, KJV).*

> *"We know that God does not hear sinners; but if anyone is God-fearing and does His will, He hears him" (John 9:31, NASB).*

These *scriptures* have very strong words for those who deceive themselves into thinking they are without sin. Do not deceive yourselves.

> *"But if ye will not do so, behold, ye have sinned against the* Lord*: and be sure your sin will find you out" (Num. 32:23, KJV).*

> *"But your iniquities have separated you from your God; and your sins have hidden His face from you, so that He will not hear" (Isa. 59:2, NIV).*

As you can see, *our Father* validates *His* stance on concealing sin or not confessing sin. This is the same difference.

For the sake of simplicity, as you study and apply *His* Word, *the Father* will honor your commitment to change.

Additionally, *He* will give divine direction on areas within your life to yield *His* best for you. Be prepared. This will not be a pleasant experience most of the time.

Your ultimate goal should be to reflect the image of Jesus Christ. As you grow in grace (*and this will not be overnight*), *the Father* will give divine direction through *His* Word, prayer, and other believers. On another front, if you are not reflecting Jesus Christ, who are you reflecting?

If you are void of a church home at this time, I have listed a few radio and television pastors who are gifted in teaching the Word.

These are Holy Spirit–inspired radio and television pastors God uses to teach us.

To name a few, there is Pastor John MacArthur with *Grace to You Ministries,* website addresses http://www.gty.org.

There's Dr. Charles Stanley with *In Touch Ministries,* website address http://www.intouch.org.

Last, there's Dr. Michael Youssef with *Leading the Way Ministries,* website address http://www.leadingtheway.org.

The above list of pastors teaches appropriate application of *Scriptures,* without fail.

Before proceeding, I do suggest prayerfully seeking a Bible teaching church home. It is sin for you to forsake assembling with other believers, according to *Scripture.*

> "*Not forsaking the assembling of ourselves together, as the manner of some is; but exhorting one another: and so much the more, as ye see the day approaching*" (Heb. 10:25, KJV).

I have heard some believers say, "You don't have to attend church because church is in your heart." Well, sure, church maybe in your heart, but it is better to please *the Father* than yourself. Simply stated, this is a cop-out statement to self-serve. Those with this mindset have discarded what the *Scripture* clearly states to serve *the Father* their way. Besides, it would not be beneficial to forfeit a growing relationship with *the Father*. Your obedience and submission to *His* will is the only thing acceptable to a *Holy God*. Remember, any sin (small or great) separates us from *our Father*.

He does not concern *Himself* with our petty and meaningless excuses; *He* only cares about *His* glory. If you ignore what *His* Word commands you to do, you are living in rebellion and opposition to a *Holy God*. This is not a good thing. I know the above statement is blunt, but it is the real truth. Within the *Old Testament* and *New Testament*, God did not tolerate sin. Actually, before Jesus came on the scene, in the *New Testament* Books, the Israelites were judged over and over again for their sin.

Plus, you will be recharged and reinforced in your efforts to seek *His* mind, and truth.

And you will be challenged to step out of your comfort zone to grow. *The Father* does not want us to be ignorant of *His* Word.

Many suffer due to lack of knowledge regarding the *Word of God* because they do not study, or if they do study, but some do not apply the Word to their lives. Therefore, many in Christendom continue to live in complete self-deception and carnality.

> *"My people are destroyed for lack of knowledge: because thou hast rejected knowledge, I will also reject thee, that thou shalt be no priest to me: seeing thou hast forgotten the law of thy God, I will also forget thy children"* (Hosea 4:6, KJV).

When *His* Word is studied and the *Holy Spirit* has revealed to you things in your life that need to be adjusted or eliminated, you must adhere.

This is why *He* left the Bible for us to study to show ourselves approved, rightly dividing the word of truth. It is an outright sin for anyone who professed to be a born-again believer not to study the *Scriptures,* myself included.

Do you remember the old cliché, "This book will keep you from sin, and sin will keep you from this book"? I know this is a made-up tale, but it is very true.

So if the above statement applies to you, this is an opportunity to confess your sin, ask forgiveness, and move forward *His* way.

> *"Study to shew thyself approved unto God, a workman that needeth not to be ashamed, rightly dividing the word of truth"* (2 Tim. 2:15, KJV).

Sadly, many within the body of Christ, who have professed to be Christians do not pick up a Bible until Sunday morning.

So they do not know if the pastor is preaching or teaching the truth or not!

Beloved, if you do not study and apply *Scriptures* to your daily life, *you will not grow.*

I believe this is why so many believers are "still on milk" within our congregations.

> *"For everyone who partakes only of milk is not accustomed to the word of righteousness, for he is an infant"* (Heb. 5:13, KJV).

Unfortunately, many pastors are left with the burden of teaching and preaching to a congregation who refuses to grow up and mature. Also, if you are not maturing biblically or spiritually, how can you witness to the lost?

How can you be a functional part of the true vine? To clarify, Jesus is the true vine, and *our Father* is the husbandman (owner of the land in biblical times or farmer).

In those days when Jesus walked the earth, farming was an essential part of life for the people. How can you know your pastor is teaching the truth? For the sake of obtaining a real understanding, please study and restudy the following *scriptures*:

"*I am the true vine, and my Father is the husbandman.*

"*Every branch in me that beareth not fruit he taketh away: and every branch that beareth fruit, he purgeth it, that it may bring forth more fruit.*

"*Now ye are clean through the word which I have spoken unto you.*

"*Abide in me, and I in you. As the branch cannot bear fruit of itself, except it abide in the vine; no more can ye, except ye abide in me.*

"*I am the vine, ye are the branches: He that abideth in me, and I in him, the same bringeth forth much fruit: for without me ye can do nothing.*

"*If a man abide not in me, he is cast forth as a branch, and is withered; and men gather them, and cast them into the fire, and they are burned*" (John 15, KJV).

The above *scriptures* beg the question, are you really born again? Are you submitted to obedience to the *Scriptures*? I am not talking about just the *scriptures* you like but *all scriptures*.

Beloved, it is not my intent to be harsh in any way, but I am attempting to provoke you to think in the space of reality. Are you bearing spiritual fruit?

Are you really abiding in Jesus Christ?

According to the *scriptures* listed above, if you are not abiding in Christ or producing fruit, what's going on with you? The *Scriptures* state you must abide in *Him* or what you are producing is not of *Him* and will be "*cast into the fire.*" The reason I ask you such a deep questions is because if indeed this applies to you, you are wasting valuable time. You are merely mocking time. You see, we have to do it *His* way, not ours. Besides, our way does not work.

Beloved, please understand, there is a vast difference of abiding in Christ and bonding a relationship with *Him* as opposed to attending church.

Many churchgoers have the misconception that if they are a member of a church congregation, *they are abiding in Christ*. This is simply not true. Actually, there are many who attend church regularly who are not saved or living in disobedience to *His* word.

I know this analogy sounds almost inconceivable. To clarify, one has to be born-again through Jesus Christ in order to abide in Christ and baptized with the *Holy Spirit*.

> *"He said to them, 'Did you receive the Holy Spirit when you believed?' And they said to him, 'No, we have not even heard whether there is a Holy Spirit'" (Acts 19:2 NASB).*

If you are wondering why you need the *Holy Spirit*, please read the following:

Jesus said that we would *"receive power when the Holy Spirit comes upon you"* in Acts 1:8 and power to live holy lives, power to witness, power to pray, to understand scripture, to minister, and to lay our lives down (Acts 9:17–20; John 16:14; Luke 24:24; Rom. 8:26).

The *Holy Spirit* is to be received by all believers so that they can receive, with the power, certain "gifts" from God: the gifts of healing, power wisdom, power in faith, power in knowledge, power in miracles, and power to speak the truth of God. In other words, the *Holy Spirit* is received to receive power to be active "Body of Christ" ministering in the earth today and as long as you live. The apostle Paul said for us to "earnestly desire spiritual gifts" (1 Cor. 12:31, 14:1).

If you are sure you are a believer and also are willing to obey God in your life and then ask for the *Holy Spirit* to enter your life, to take up residence, and to fill and cleanse you with *His* heavenly fire (Matt. 3:11), *"your heavenly father will give the Holy Spirit to them that ask of Him"* (Luke 11:13).

The Baptism of the Holy Spirit is for now and has always been available for any believer bold enough to trust God and obey Him. When the believers asked for advice from the apostles on the day of Pentecost, *they were told to "repent," "be baptized," and "receive the Holy Spirit"* (Acts 2:38). Jesus said in *His* Sermon on the Mount,

"Blessed are they who hunger and thirst after righteousness; for they shall be filled" (Matt. 5:6).

In order to live out *His* commandments, as listed above, I have provided a way to resolve this dilemma for you by divine inspiration. If you are not sure about your salvation, I included *scripture* passages below to assist you with accepting Jesus Christ as your personal Savior:

- *Acknowledge* that *Jesus* has not been first in your life and ask Him to forgive your sins.

  "If we confess our sins He is faithful and just to forgive us our sins, and to cleanse us from all unrighteousness" (1 John 1:9).

- *Believe* that Jesus died to pay for your sins and that He rose again and is alive today.

  "That if though shalt confess with thy mouth the Lord Jesus, and shalt believe in thine heart that God hath raised Him from the dead, though shalt be saved" (Rom. 10:9).

- *Accept* God's free gift of salvation. Don't try to earn it.

  "For by grace are ye saved through faith; and that not of yourselves: it is a free gift of God: Not of works, lest any man should boast" (Eph. 2:8–9).

- *Allow* Jesus Christ to come into your life and be the Lord ("director") of your life.

  "But as man as received Him, to them gave He power to become the sons of God, even to them that believe on His name: Which were born, not or blood, nor of the will of the flesh, nor of the will of man, but of

God" (John 1:12–13) (http://www.dayspringfamilychurch.org/pages.asp?pageid=10529).

I included salvation *scriptures* simply because I cannot assume everyone who reads this book is born-again. And the major reason for salvation inclusion is *I have no desire to offend the Father by not offering His free gift of salvation.*

I am hopeful these words are soothing to your mind and heart. Please say an earnest, heartfelt prayer to accept Jesus as your personal savior. Beloved, you will know *He* has accepted your plea because *the Father* will confirm acceptance within your heart. Pray the scriptures listed by the item "Believe." accept and allow *Him* to come into your heart.

Now after you have done the above prayer, eternal life is your destination. You have made the most important decision ever to be made in your life, which has eternal consequences. To interpret, now you are on your way to heaven when before you were on your way to eternal damnation. The thought of not being sure where you are going after death has been resolved. Of course, if you are already born again, I commend you.

Going forward, the main priority for you should be reevaluating whether or not you are abiding with *Jesus Christ*. If not, the earlier writings will be of assistance in helping you to get this right. The *scriptures* are the final authority, not what I say.

Beloved, there is no need to be ashamed or aggravated about your circumstances. The beautiful thing is *He* is a forgiving *Father* who will earnestly help you through this.

Remember, *"we all have fallen short of the glory of God,"* according to Rom. 3:23.

The keyword is *all*. This means I have fallen short of *His* glory. So have your pastor, your family members, friends, and associates.

It does not matter how religious or how well someone knows the Bible, they are not without sin. It does not matter if an individual is a pillar in the community or has achieved high pedigree within our society.

There is only one being who has ever walked the earth who was without sin, and his name was and is Jesus. So don't be fooled by how good people appear to be; it is merely an illusion. Without a personal growing relationship with *Jesus Christ,* it is impossible for any one of us to be good.

You see, all humans have a natural inclination to sin without thinking about it.

Our natural propensity to sin goes back to the Garden of Eve in the book of Genesis. Every human born after the fall of man or Adam and Eve are born with a sinful nature, which is not controllable unless we have a submitted will to *our Creator, God the Father.* Please study Genesis 3:1–24 to learn when and where all the confusion of sin began. Also, the rest of the *Old Testament books* document an ongoing inability for man to control his sinful nature. Naturally, man desires to have his way, even if he is warned that his way will lead to destruction. Plus, man believes his way to be right.

> *"There is a way which seems right to a man, But its end is the way of death"* (Prov. 14:12, NASB).

You know how some people will suggest for you to do something they themselves have not done? Please know, all the biblical instructions I have written, I have done them too. What I am saying is, the things I am suggesting you to do throughout this book, I have done myself.

Blessed be the name of the Lord! *He* is a forgiving and merciful *Father*, who is waiting for you to surrender. *He* extends unmerited grace to each of us, even if we don't deserve *His* grace. Oh, glory to our Heavenly Father, whose grace abounds in tender mercies toward *His* people! You see, there is always hope. Beloved, you are not like the world (or people who do not know Jesus), who is without hope in their walk.

> *"Brothers and sisters, we do not want you to be uninformed about those who sleep in death, so that you do not grieve like the rest of mankind, who have no hope"* (1 Thess. 4:13, NIV).

Are you aware the angels rejoice when one sinner repents of his or her sins?

> *"Likewise, I say unto you, there is joy in the presence of the angels of God over one sinner that repenteth"* (Luke 15:10, KJV).

On another front, I am still an avid student of the infallible, inherent Word of God. I believe the Bible is the absolute truth, and I cannot get enough of the spiritual food the Bible provides for my soul. I have a thirst for *His* Word that nothing else will quench, and I mean nothing. There are many things to fall in love with in this world, but please allow me to suggest to you a new love. For the sake of your family, future generations, and your circle of influence, fall in love with Jesus Christ and *His* infallible Word. Beloved, you will never be the same person ever again. There will be spiritual growth beyond what you ever imagined. You see, when one makes a conscientious choice or decision to live in obedience, by default, life as you know it changes. Beloved, you will begin to see beyond your world and have a global prospective. As human beings, we have limitations. That said, in our natural condition, there is only so far we can travel mentally due to our natural limitations. However, in the spiritual realm (when born-again and being endowed with the power of the Holy Spirit), you no longer look at life from a natural prospective.

Thus, you have become a new creation in Jesus Christ, and all things will become new.

> *"Therefore, if anyone is in Christ, he is a new creation; old things have passed away; behold, all things have become new"* (2 Cor. 5:17, NKJV).

Now this revelation should be great news to you. Rejoice and share the good news!

Beloved, you are well on your way to a new life of knowing real peace and unexplainable fellowship with *the Father*.

Whether you are a babe in Christ or a new believer, a seasoned believer, or somewhere in between, you have been inspired to grow.

I have purposely challenged you to leave old thought processes behind and embrace the new life.

Although you may or may not realize it, you will inspire others inside and outside of your circle to seek a growing relationship with Christ. This is good.

I am grateful *He* has chosen me to be a part of the healing process to assist you with moving forward.

Sometimes change is not easy, especially when one has been doing things the same way for many years or even decades. With that said, if you make a decision to be committed, obedient, and submitted to *our Creator, He* can open doors no one can close, and *He* can close doors no one can open.

> *"I know your works: behold, I have set before you an open door, and no man can shut it: for you have a little strength, and have kept my word, and have not denied my name"* (Rev. 3:8, KJV).

I am not referring to just a physical door, but I am referring to physical and spiritual doors because the *Scriptures* are referring to both. Although I will say, *the Father* has absolute power to do the same with a physical door if *He* chooses to do so because I have experienced *His* divine intervention of keeping the door to a new career position open for me, and no one could stop it from happening.

Do you desire *His* best? I realize this is a rhetorical question; I am sure your answer is yes. I have provided biblical principles by which you can achieve *His* best for yourself and help to inspire others by choosing to live an obedient life.

This book is not very long, so you can mark up the pages liberally for future reference.

I am convinced that if you study the inherent Word of God with the intent of applying *His* Word to your life, you will never be the same person.

Beloved, I am living proof that a change will come.

CHAPTER 4

Trust Our Father in Heaven

"Blessed are all they that put their trust in him" (Ps. 2:12, KJV).

As you honestly sort through your *deferred hope status,* trusting *our Father* in heaven is key. You are learning that turning to *Scriptures,* and our Heavenly Father is an absolute critical element in your healing process.

Many of us choose to call a friend or close relative to discuss our *deferred hope status.* Although there is nothing wrong with confiding in a close friend, please be sure your trusted friend or relative is deeply rooted in providing biblical advice.

If not, well-intentioned friends or relatives advice could potentially cause more issues for you. Many times over, more issues are exactly what happen by default.

For the sake of clarification, when believers obtain personal advice from ungodly people, the devil has his opportunity to slyly slip in to spin evil webs. This is why I do not advise seeking advice from ungodly counsel, which can sometimes be in the form of family or friends. Yes, I did say that.

Unfortunately for many within the *body of Christ,* this route is chosen. Thus, the unbridled chaos begins in their lives at full speed. And let me tell you, only *the Father* has the divine power to fix any of your problems, not humans.

I am not saying humans cannot fix or give advice on human issues, I am just suggesting to you to be very careful.

As human beings, we have mental limitations or lack divine insight for *His* perfect will. Unless the council is born again and led by the *Holy Spirit*, it would be ill-advised.

According to the following *scriptures*, we were never meant to follow our thinking or our own understanding at all.

Please study the *scriptures* below and ask *Him* to plant this truth in your heart.

> *"Trust in the LORD with all your heart; And do not lean on your own understanding.*
> *"In all your ways acknowledge Him, And He will make your paths straight" (Prov. 3:5–6, NASB).*

It is challenging for every born-again believer to put into practice praying and seeking God's mind for answers or seeking biblical counseling. This is absolutely necessary to build faith.

The above comment may seem far removed, but unfortunately, many of us do not seek the *Scriptures* or God first.

We forget what *He* said to us:

> *"Come to Me, all you who labor and are heavy laden, and I will give you rest. Take My yoke upon you and learn from Me, for I am gentle and lowly in heart, and you will find rest for your souls. For My yoke is easy and My burden is light"* (Matt. 11:28–30, NASB).

What are the reasons keeping you from seeking God's mind? Do you panic? Are you afraid of *His* Word? Or do you still desire to follow *Him* your way?

Many believers are afraid to seek *His* mind or study *His* Word, so they panic and do nothing.

I am discussing churchgoing folks here too.

I believe I addressed in chapter 3 that if you pray to *the Father* earnestly to seek revelation of *His* Word, *He* will endow you with the gift of the *Holy Spirit* to be your spiritual teacher of *His* Word.

Beloved, hopefully you realize doing things your way is no longer an option at this point.

However, if panicking is a normal part of your reaction to conflict or difficulties, this must change today. To panic or ignore *the Father's* Word due to fear or whatever else that maybe paralyzing you is displaying lack of faith.

Simply stated, panicking is not what *He* has called us to do. *Our Father in heaven* has not given us a spirit of fear, which is the root of going into panic mode.

I have had countless relatives and friends (who are professed believers) over the years that were paralyzed with fear to do this or that. In most cases, *the Father* was directing them biblically to carry out certain things in their lives. Even when I would show them what the *Scriptures* said about fear and prayed with them, still some would remain stuck.

Now this is the point: many miss out on *His* blessings due to fear and disobedience. Because if the *Scriptures* command us not to embrace fear as an attribute, then we should not do it; it is that simple. Since we are biblically commanded not to hold on to fear, if we continue to do so, we are then operating in the status of disobedience.

> *"For God has not given us a spirit of fear, but of power and of love and of a sound mind" (1 Tim. 1:7, NASB).*

What happened to your faith in God along the way? *Scriptures* that are very helpful in building faith are known within Christendom as "the faith; Hall of Fame."

Study at your leisure Hebrews 11, and you will be biblically enlightened how the saints of old were able to trust *our Father*, although they could not see the end.

When I was struggling with building faith and trusting God completely, I studied and pondered over Hebrews 11.

WHAT TO DO WHEN HOPE IS DEFERRED

Please study about how Abraham left his home country of Canaan to go to an unknown country God had directed him to. Can you imagine in the twenty-first century someone telling you to leave your home to start over?

> *"By faith Able offered a more excellent sacrifice than Cain, by which he obtained witness that he was righteous, God testifying of his gifts: and by it he being dead yet speaks" (Heb. 11:4, KJV).*

Study how Noah built an ark when there was no forecast of rain.

> *"By faith Noah, being warned of God of things not seen as yet, move with fear, prepared an ark to the saving of his house; by the which he condemned the world, and became heir of the righteousness which is by faith" (Heb. 11:7, KJV).*

Abraham went to a foreign land divinely directed.

> *"By faith Abraham, when he was called to go out into a place which he should after receive for an inheritance, obeyed; and he went out, not knowing where he went" (Heb. 11:8, KJV).*

> *"By faith he sojourned in the land of promise, as in a strange country, dwelling in tabernacles with Isaac and Jacob, the heirs with him of the same promise" (Heb 11:9, KJV).*

> *"By faith Enoch was translated that he should not see death; and was not found, because God had translated him: for before his translation he had this testimony, that he pleased God" (Heb. 11:5, KJV).*

Do you desire that your testimony please God?

And the true biblical stories of faith in Hebrews 11 go on and on.

The *scripture* below addresses the very essence of why we as believers must embrace a faith-bearing mindset:

> *"But without faith it is impossible to please him: for he that comes to God must believe that he is, and that he is a rewarder of them that diligently seek him"* (Heb. 11:6, KJV).

The above *scripture* begs the question, do you really have faith?

Actually, the *scriptures* written above challenge you by forcing self-examination for the existence of true faith. Sometimes many believers think they have faith until a major life-altering crisis occurs in their lives. When this happens, it is truly a faith test.

Unfortunately, for many of us, turning to *the Father* for immediate help is not our first reaction. In the past, I am guilty of going within myself for help, only to find I have human limitations, just as everyone else does.

Of course, when my human limitations were blaring back at me, I would turn to *our Father* for divine help. I am reminded of an old spiritual song, "What a Friend We Have in Jesus." I used to sing it at Growing Valley Baptist Church in Longview, Texas.

> *"What a friend we have in Jesus, all our sins and griefs to bear!*
> *What a privilege to carry everything to God in prayer!*
> *O what peace we often forfeit, O what needless pain we bear, all because we do not carry everything to God in prayer.*
> *Have we trials and temptations? Is there trouble anywhere?*
> *We should never be discouraged; take it to the Lord in prayer.*

Can we find a friend so faithful who will all our sorrows share?

Jesus knows our every weakness; take it to the Lord in prayer.

Are we weak and heavy laden, cumbered with a load of care?

Precious Savior, still our refuge; take it to the Lord in prayer.

Do thy friends despise, forsake thee? Take it to the Lord in prayer!

In his arms he'll take and shield thee; thou wilt find a solace there."

This song was written by Joseph M. Scriven in 1855 to comfort his mother who lived in Ireland, but was very ill (http://suite101.com/article/what-a-friend-we-have-in-jesus-a57293).

In my earlier years, I wish I had known to take everything to *Him* in prayer. I am certain I bore needless pain and stress because I did not have the faith to lay it all down at *His* feet. Now I clearly understand why the old folks use sing the song listed above all the time.

I am posing another question: did you give up on the Lord?

Sometimes, giving up on the Lord occurs when we trust ourselves and our own minds. Actually, I have discovered over time that it can be detrimental to trust my own intellect.

You see, without trusting in *the Father's* divine wisdom through prayer and *Scripture* application, there will be failure. To make it plain, failure is imminent.

The Father never forces us to trust *Him*. However, as followers of Christ, *He* gives clear and concise guidance. The *Scriptures* give us a clear path to the kind of faith and trust we are supposed to exhibit at all times.

Please study and apply the following *scriptures*:

> *"Those who know your name will trust in you, for you, LORD, have never forsaken those who seek you"* (Ps. 9:10, KJV).

> *"Some trust in chariots and some in horses, but we trust in the name of the LORD" (Ps. 20:7, KJV).*
>
> *"The LORD is my strength and my shield; my heart trusts in him, and I am helped. My heart leaps for joy and I will give thanks to him in song" (Ps. 28:7, KJV).*
>
> *"But I trust in you, O LORD; I say, "You are my God" (Ps. 31:14 KJV).*

Beloved, the biblical principles within this chapter will be instrumental in gradually changing the way you think about your "*deferred hope status.*"

If you make a choice today to permit the biblical references to permeate into your heart, soul, and mind, this is your help.

The Father blesses each believer with a free will. Our free will is addressed within the *Scriptures* as "liberty."

> *"Now the Lord is that Spirit: and where the Spirit of the Lord is, there is liberty" (2 Cor. 3:17, KJV).*

What is the definition of *liberty*? *Merriam-Webster online* defines *liberty* as "the power of choice."

Basically, we can do as we please; however, there are always going to be divine consequences for ungodly choices, so be sure to make choices or exercise liberties that are biblically aligned, thereby pleasing *our Creator* and preventing the devil from gaining a foothold within your life.

In essence, every believer has been given a free will by *our Creator* to choose what is biblical or not. *He* never forces us to make the right decisions or choices. You read what happened to Adam in Eve in the book of Genesis, right? Please study at your leisure for a refresher in free will gone wrong in Genesis 3.

Truth be told, Adam and Eve's fall was the beginning of every human being struggle to do what is right naturally.

Although I will say, if you are spiritually connected to *the Father with a growing personal relationship*, *He* will divinely orchestrate circumstances to intervene for you.

One very important point to consider, every man or woman born, whether born-again or not, has internal knowledge of right and wrong.

The evidence to prove all humans have internal knowledge is people naturally judge what is right or wrong daily. These very clear and concise actions validate that an individual does know the difference.

It does not matter if a person claims to be an atheist. If you take the time to observe their natural behavior, you will see for yourself.

This camp knows there is a sovereign *Creator*; however, due to staunch denial, they cling on to their false beliefs, which ultimately destroy them.

Thereby, the nonbeliever proves he or she knows the difference between right or wrong by their own actions! Take time to observe anyone who states he or she does not believe in the God of the Bible.

Who do nonbelievers or atheists call on the minute there is a major catastrophic event such as 9/11 or Hurricane Katrina? Or to make it even more personal, when a very close family member passes away, who is called on for divine help?

With that said, many still choose to go their own way. I elaborated in great detail within chapter 3 the ongoing fallout many within the *body of Christ* endure due to doing things "their way."

There is an advantage in submitting your will in all areas of your life to *our Savior*. *The Father* knows what is good for you. *He* has demonstrated *His* divine commitment for *His* glory throughout creation of the universe and mankind.

> *"And one cried unto another, and said, Holy, holy, holy, is the LORD of hosts: the whole earth is full of his glory"* (Isa. 6:3, KJV).

> *"The heavens declare the glory of God; and the firmament sheweth his handywork"* (Ps. 19:1, KJV).

As you can see, even all *His* creations declare *His* glory! God never has to ask the wind to blow; nor does *He* ever ask the sea to produce waves and so on. Beloved, what more proof do you need?

The *God of the Bible* is *the Creator* of this awesome universe. We mere humans marvel in total awe over *His* handiwork.

Many within the scientific community have done their absolute best to disprove *He* created the universe, only to be met with utter defeat and submission.

Read an excerpt from the following article entitled "Scientific Proof that God Exists" written by Craig Hamilton. The excerpt deals with the idea of how far off the map some scientists are willing to travel in order to make their frivolous points.

Amit Goswami is a professor of physics at the University of Oregon and a member of the university's Institute of Theoretical Science.

> *"Interviewing Amit Goswami was a mind-bending and concept-challenging experience. Listening to him explain many ideas with which he seemed perfectly at home, required, for me, such a suspension of disbelief that I at times found myself having to stretch far beyond anything I had previously considered. (Goswami is also a great fan of science fiction whose first book, The Cosmic Dancers, was a look at science fiction through the eyes of a physicist.)" (http://www.enlightennext.org/magazine/j11/goswami.asp).*

At your leisure, please take time to read the entire interview; it is totally mind-boggling to read. The highly educated professor is no doubt an intellectual with advanced abilities to reason the unexplainable theories within the complex human mind.

Professor Goswami is among a growing number of theorists who go to great lengths to disprove there is not a divine *Creator*. Goswami's theory, simply stated, is mysticism and spirituality.

These types are generally highly educated and hold advanced degrees in various fields of education from science, physics, astronomy, and so on. It is almost comical to believe these guys actually trust in such faulty and unsubstantiated human dogma.

But it is true.

The nonbelieving physicists and scientists of our world are not alone in their belief systems.

There are hundreds, if not thousands, of websites dedicated to disproving the God of the Bible exist. Some are written from the point of view of atheists, scientists, evolutionists, and the like. There is one website in particular I discovered with a complete breakdown by percentages of scientists and educators who hold advanced degrees who do not believe in God. The scientists and educators of higher learning institutions hold advanced degrees in physics, chemistry, biology, sociology, economics, political science, and psychology.

It is almost inconceivable to think these highly educated people do not believe God exist. The website's creator, Rich Deem, wrote an objective article entitled "Why Are Most Scientist Atheist if There Is Evidence for Belief in God?" Mr. Deem's present the facts based on a twentieth century study and survey of highly educated professionals. I think it is interesting to learn how some think on the other side of the camp. Actually, studying atheistic point of views when it comes to nonbelief in the God of the Bible has given me great insight on how to witness to them from an educated position of their belief systems. Should I be placed in a position to do so, I have to be prepared to give in answer regarding the "hope that is within me." This is an excellent read, which I highly recommend. Mr. Deem's wrote this assessment from a totally unbiased standpoint while presenting the facts. There are countless other links on this website to educate you regarding the other side of the fence of nonbelievers. I personally believe the site was created to be instrumental in building apologetics for believers who are called to witness to this sect.

I have discovered there are some within the *body of Christ* who believe and teach that God and *His* Word are not the final authority. Who would have thought there would be such a movement in the twenty-first century?

There are many facets to the rejection of God and the Bible as the final authority and inherent Word of God.

Some within our modern society openly dispute God's biblical design for all humanity.

For instance, there are countless religions established or created that deny the deity of Christ. There are some who embrace staunch beliefs and doctrine to support their claims (i.e., Islam, Buddhism, Hinduism, Gnosticism, Scientology, and mysticism, etc.); however, these religions are blasphemous. This is not a complete list.

I will not venture too deeply into this subject matter because I only desire to make the point of how other religions undermine belief and trust in the Bible. Therefore, these rapidly growing and thriving religions are causing many in our progressive society to venture into a mind-set of trusting false authorities and becoming confused. Thus, disbelief and distrust in the *God of the Bible* and *His* written authority, the Bible, has become more common in America. God is God; it is settled in heaven.

Moving right along, regardless of what man thinks or believes, his limited thought processes are just that—limited. In man's arrogance (this verbiage includes women, as well), he believes that he should be worshiped and honored. To prove my point, look at many fallen ministers or pastors who were unexpectedly exposed on a national or international level.

You see, *our Father* created each one of us to reflect *His* likeness.

Simply stated, God created man to give *Him* glory and to serve only *Him*. The *scripture* address this issue in the Ten Commandments, written in the book of Exodus.

> "*Thou shalt have no other gods before me*" *(Exod. 20:3, KJV)*.

The Father will not compete with false religions or false gods. I would suggest, at your leisure, to study the Old Testament in an effort to gain a biblical prospective on God's view on putting other things before *Him* and the consequences this can and will bring forth. Many within the *body of Christ* suffer and are destroyed needlessly due to lack of knowledge.

> *"My people are destroyed for lack of knowledge: because thou hast rejected knowledge, I will also reject thee, that thou shalt be no priest to me: seeing thou hast forgotten the law of thy God, I will also forget thy children"* (Hosea 4:6, KJV).

Unfortunately, there are believers who attend church on a regular basis who knowingly reject the *Scriptures*. It is hard to believe this sort of thing is occurring, but it is. Why do you think there is so much chaos and discord within our twenty-first century church congregations? It boils down to this: in all facets of life, whether it is a churchgoing believer or the secular populous, man desires to have his way at all cost. However, when man has his own way, it causes confusion, division, and separation from God. There are always consequences for rejecting God's best.

> *"Be not deceived; God is not mocked: for whatsoever a man soweth, that shall he also reap"* (Gal. 6:7, KJV).

You see, *the Father* will not bless any person or congregation who operates in this manner. Please know when a person or church congregation is operating in discord, neither God nor the *Holy Spirit* resides or takes up residence there. The other major issue is many will not admit they are out of fellowship with *the Father* due to pride and arrogance. Basically, these congregations or people are operating under legalistic traditions, which hinder real repentance and actually fortify a very destructive stance.

Thus, the congregation will be promoting all manner of ungodly ordinances and traditions. Did I mention such ungodly behavior under minds church growth?

The aforementioned analogies do not cover the breath and width of discord. I only discussed a few potential fallouts; there are many, many more.

On another front, in order to avoid being separated from *the Father*, whether it is a church congregation or a believer, you must trust and obey *Him*. There is no other way.

> *"Some trust in chariots, and some in horses: but we will remember the name of the LORD our God"* (Ps. 20:7 KJV).

Trusting *our Father in heaven,* who is the *Creator of the universe* and who has been faithful and solvent for thousands of years, will only mean security for those who choose to submit to *His* perfect will. Do you desire *His* best for you and your family? Then I would suggest for you to submit your will to *His* will right now.

Now please understand, you will still have trials and tribulations because you are still functioning in a fallen world.

You are in this world but not of this world.

But remember this:

> *"These things I have spoken unto you, that in me ye might have peace. In the world ye shall have tribulation: but be of good cheer; I have overcome the world"* (John 16:33, KJV).

Beloved, you can make it in this life, but you must place your complete trust in *our Father.*

CHAPTER 5

No Room for Doubt

"Christ never failed to distinguish between doubt and unbelief. Doubt is can't believe; unbelief is won't believe. Doubt is honesty; unbelief is obstinacy. Doubt is looking for light; unbelief is content with darkness" (Henry Drummond).

Is there any room to doubt what *"The Creator of the universe"* Jesus, our Lord and Savior can do for you?

Let's examine doubt and some likely reasons for one to embrace such nonproductive emotions.

The *Merriam-Webster Dictionary* writes, *doubt* is to *"lack confidence in, distrust or to consider unlikely."*

When you consider *our Father* created the entire universe in six days, it stands to reason that our issues are a small part of *His* divine plan too.

Our countless emotional frailties encourage self-doubt, naturally.

To interpret, unless a believer is truly submitted to a growing relationship with Christ Jesus, he or she will succumb to his or her human limitations and sinful thoughts.

As difficult as it might be for you to believe, many within the *body of Christ* embrace carnality as if this ungodly characteristic will benefit their lives.

Carnal behavior is considered a big no-no for believers.

What is a carnal mind? A carnal-minded person is someone who focuses on pleasing their fleshly desires above what God's word has commanded them to do.

Actually, you may or may not be surprised of the believers within congregations who has embodied such a destructive characteristic.

Let's examine a few *scriptures* that discourage carnal behavior.

Please read and embrace the following *scriptures* to give yourself clear insight on what the *Scriptures* say about this:

> *"For what the law could not do, in that it was weak through the flesh, God sending his own Son in the likeness of sinful flesh, and for sin, condemned sin in the flesh: That the righteousness of the law might be fulfilled in us, who walk not after the flesh, but after the Spirit. For they that are after the flesh do mind the things of the flesh; but they that are after the Spirit the things of the Spirit. For to be carnally minded is death; but to be spiritually minded is life and peace. Because the carnal mind is enmity against God: for it is not subject to the law of God, neither indeed can be"* (Rom. 8:2–7, KJV).

The carnal mind is death to the spirit's existence within a believer. Thinking in a natural context cancels out *the Father's* ability to minister and remove sin. The person who walks according to the flesh thinks about what belongs to the flesh, and the person who walks according to the Spirit thinks about what belongs to the Spirit.

The carnal mind is death, and the spiritual mind is life and peace because the person who follows the carnal mind acts in hostility toward God and does not follow God's law, and *He* will not follow those who choose this path.

The person who is under the control of the flesh cannot please God. It is impossible due to their love of sin.

I realize this is not the analogy most people would admit to, but this is the truth for many believers, and I cannot afford to assume this is not your reality.

This is one of the main reasons there is insurmountable division within congregations. The spirit of carnality is running rampant within some churches.

Please know the ever-evolving world standards would not support the above analogy either.

Actually, our current world system embraces self-doubt, low self-esteem, human inadequacies, and a litany of other human issues.

Basically, this is accomplished by the medical community labeling people with various labels, such as *bipolar, ADHD, ADD, anxiety illnesses*, and so on.

In addition, the medical community treats these medical conditions and supposedly controls these expanding disorders with medications.

Just in case you are not familiar with the named disorders, I listed a few of them below:

> *"Bipolar disorder is an illness that causes extreme mood changes from manic episodes of very high energy to the extreme lows of depression. It is also called manic-depressive disorder.*
>
> *"This illness can cause behavior so extreme that you cannot function at work, in family or social situations, or in relationships with others. Some people with bipolar disorder become suicidal.*
>
> *"Having this disorder can make you feel helpless and hopeless. But you are not alone.*
>
> *"Talking with others who suffer from it may help you learn that there is hope for a better life. And treatment can help you get back in control"* (Bipolar Disorder Health Center; "What Is Bipolar Disorder? http://www.webmd.com/bipolar-disorder/ tc/bipolar-disorder-topic-overview).

Note, attention deficit disorder, ADD, and attention deficit/hyperactivity disorder, ADHD, mimic similar behaviors.

Adults with ADHD may have difficulty following directions, remembering information, concentrating, organizing tasks, or completing work within time limits. If these difficulties are not managed appropriately, they can cause associated behavioral, emotional, social, vocational and academic problems. Childhood ADHD—attention deficit/hyperactivity disorder—is diagnosed after a child has shown six or more specific symptoms of inattention or hyperactivity on a regular basis for more than six months in more than two settings. There is no single test for ADHD.

> A doctor can diagnose ADHD with the help of specific guidelines or criteria. The diagnosis of ADHD involves the gathering of information from several sources. The doctor will consider how a child's behavior compares with that of other children the same age (Bipolar Disorder Health Center; Childhood in ADHD; http://www.webmd.com/add-adhd/childhood-adhd/ast_oneadhd-children).

With that said, who is the most likely sect to benefit from prescribing disorder medications to the masses just within these United States of America?

I think you see where I am going with this.

The medical professionals or psychologists who prescribe the medicines and the pharmaceutical giants who manufacture the drugs are the benefactors of large profits.

For the sake of fairness to the medical and the psychology community, there are many people (some believers) who absolutely must be on daily medications. I make this statement because unfortunately.

There is much to be said about believers seeking secular-minded solutions to resolve spiritual problems. The medical community is in the business of medicating sin, which is impossible.

I personally have relatives who must be medicated daily, or else they cannot function or it is impossible to deal with them.

Let's reason for a minute.

Many of our nation's ills or plagues are born from sin. You will not hear this stated within any public forum. Hopefully you are familiar with the countless plagues and diseases that were disseminated to the Israelites and others throughout the *Old Testament*.

Many times over, disobedience and sin caused the masses in the *Old Testament* days to endure plagues and disease, and I submit to you the same is true for our current generation.

I realize this sort of biblical analogy is not taught in mainstream church congregations for various reasons. Unfortunately, many churchgoing folks would not believe it anyway.

Many who are seated in the church pews every Sunday do not study the Bible for their own enlightenment of what the *Scriptures* say about sin.

Be mindful, I am referring to the folks who do not trust *our Father* to heal them of medical issues, insecurities, and other inadequacies. Many of these folks seek man as their sole healer. Of course, people who seek man as their ultimate healer will be disappointed. Man does not have the ability to spiritually heal himself unless the Father heals, let alone you, beloved.

The *God of the Bible* inspired a spiritual rejuvenation road map called the Bible, which is the biblical method that *all* our human issues can be addressed.

The Father never intended for believers to seek help outside of consulting *Him* and the *scriptures*. However, there are many within the *Body of Christ* take this heavily-traveled road, and eventually hurt themselves.

This usually occurs when there is lack of faith or no faith in *The Father's* divine ability to care for them. I wrote in chapter 4 about not having faith, which makes it impossible to please *God*. Beloved, *He* only honors faith in *Him*, nothing else.

Doubting God is another word for *unbelief, lack of trust,* and *lack of faith*.

Please study and apply the following *scriptures,* as follows:

> *"Jesus immediately reached out his hand and took hold of him, saying to him, "O you of little faith, why did you doubt" (Matt. 14:31, ESV).*
>
> *"And have mercy on those who doubt" (Jude 1:22, ESV).*
>
> *"But let him ask in faith, with no doubting, for the one who doubts is like a wave of the sea that is driven and tossed by the wind" (James 1:6, ESV).*
>
> *"And Jesus answered them, 'Truly, I say to you, if you have faith and do not doubt, you will not only do what has been done to the fig tree, but even if you say to this mountain, "Be taken up and thrown into the sea," it will happen'" (Matt. 21:21, ESV).*
>
> *"Behold, He who that is able to keep Israel; and who does not slumber or sleep" (Ps. 121:4, NASB).*

And *He* still keeps all of us who are living within the twenty-first century and beyond if we let *Him*. Although we are gentiles, we have accepted *Jesus* as our personal savior, and we belong to *Him*.

Beloved, when doubt, unbelief, lack of trust, or faith begin to creep up within your psyche, thrust your mind forcefully back to all the blessings *He* has miraculously done in your life. *Our Father* is our faithful pastor as we commune with *Him*. I must say, even seasoned believers who lose focus has moments of doubt in the Lord's capabilities at some point and time. The keywords here are *losing focus*.

I believe doubt is born of our own sinful nature. Many of us still desire to trust in ourselves, which is our natural way of thinking.

It is sometimes easier for some of us think, naturally opposed to delving into our spiritual minds. Could it be there is a measure of self-pity?

I am provoking food for your thought processes to assist you in where you are or where you may be headed.

Our spiritual minds consist of the thinking process that the *Holy Spirit* has revealed *God's* Word to us while studying and applying *His* precepts.

As one grows in grace, by constantly studying and applying *the Word* over time and living an obedient life, he will begin to think with his spiritual mind.

Actually, this is the spiritual goal for all born-again believers. Because the closer one becomes to Jesus, the more he or she will aspire to be like *Him*.

Thus, mirroring Christ-like behavior; a maturing believer in Christ will doubt less; thereby, being a visible and illuminate example to others.

I can tell you from experience; this spiritual transformation is not something, which will occur overnight or within a short period of time.

I have been in the Christian faith for many, many years, and I still have moments of doubt. Of course, when I realize what I am doing, I confess my unbelief immediately.

I believe constant self-evaluation will be the simplest method to remain on top of this issue. Let's not forget, confession of sins is paramount as well.

All human beings; and I reiterate *all*, which were born after the fall of Adam and Eve are born with a *natural* sinful.

Therefore, sin is the cause of every human being to have limitations, with the exception of *Jesus*.

> *"And the Word became flesh, and dwelt among us, and we saw His glory, glory as of the only begotten from the Father, full of grace and truth" (John 1:14, NASB).*

Jesus (God-man) was the only man ever born without sin or a sinful nature.

> *"For he hath made him to be sin for us, who knew no sin; that we might be made the righteousness of God in him" (2 Cor. 5:21, KJV).*

> *"You know that he appeared in order to take away sins, and in him there is no sin" (1 John 3:5, KJV).*

Jesus Christ is a deity who was divinely sent to earth by *His Father* (*God*) to die for our sins. You see, *the Father* cannot look upon sin. Therefore, Jesus was a divine acceptable substitute sent to earth to die for all mankind. We were all lost in our trespasses and sin.

> *"And you hath he quickened, who were dead in trespasses and sins" (Eph. 2:1).*

For the sake of clarification, within the *Old Testament*, there are countless *scriptures* validating the necessity for animal sacrifices to God by the Prophets of old on behalf of the Israelites as temporary substitute for their sins.

> *"And all its fat he shall remove as the fat of the lamb is removed from the sacrifice of peace offerings, and the priest shall burn it on the altar, on top of the Lord's food offerings. And the priest shall make atonement for him for the sin which he has committed, and he shall be forgiven" (Lev. 4:35, ESV).*

> *"Then he shall offer the second for a burnt offering according to the rule. And the priest shall make atonement for him for the sin that he has committed, and he shall be forgiven" (Lev. 5:10, ESV).*

According to Hebrews 9:22, *the Father* is clear, without the shedding of blood, there is no remission of sins.

> *"And almost all things are by the law purged with blood; and without shedding of blood is no remission" (Heb. 9:22, KJV).*

Of course, Jesus was the New Testament blood sacrifice for our past and present sins. Beloved, I hope you have developed a clear understanding of the underlying cause for doubt and other sinful ailments humanity struggles with.

You see, the more submitted an obedient believer grows in grace, the keener he or she becomes of their sinful nature. We all have sinned and fell short of the "glory of God," but we must admit this failure to *Him* and ourselves honestly.

> *"For all have sinned, and come short of the glory of God" (Rom. 3:23, KJV).*

It does not matter if the believer is a pastor, teacher, deacon, or a regular churchgoer. We all struggle with all types of sin daily. This is why I stress to you throughout this book to study the Bible, pray, and live an obedient life according to the *Scriptures*.

Beloved, if you choose to go through this very difficult walk without the aforementioned biblical points, your life will show it.

Thus, your life will be very hard and all manner of sin will exist in your world.

You will always have doubts about everything? Did I say if you choose to ignore biblical principles, there is a possibility you can become reprobate?

According to *Dictionary.com*, *reprobate* means "a depraved and unprincipled; rejected by God and void of any hope of salvation."

This cannot be a good thing for anyone; however, many have chosen this destructive path.

> *"And even as they did not like to retain God in their knowledge, God gave them over to a reprobate mind, to do those things which are not convenient" (Rom. 1:28, KJV).*

> *"Examine yourselves, whether ye be in the faith; prove your own selves. Know ye not your own selves,*

how that Jesus Christ is in you, except ye be reprobates" (2 Cor. 13:5, KJV).

"Now I pray to God that ye do no evil; not that we should appear approved, but that ye should do that which is honest, though we be as reprobates" (2 Cor. 13:7, KJV).

"Now as Jannes and Jambres withstood Moses, so do these also resist the truth: men of corrupt minds, reprobate concerning the faith" (2 Tim. 3:8, KJV).

"They profess that they know God; but in works they deny him, being abominable, and disobedient, and unto every good work reprobate" (Titus 1:16, KJV).

These types have a form of godliness but deny the power of God.

"Having a form of godliness, but denying the power thereof: from such turn away" (2 Tim. 3:5, KJV).

A form of godliness is when people are religious and externally appear to be godly men before others, but in secret or behind closed doors, they constantly plotting evil.

I provided the above *scriptures* for immediate insight into God's mind regarding people who are pretending to be angels of light.

"No wonder, for even Satan disguises himself as an angel of light" (2 Cor. 11:14, NASB).

The *scriptures* listed above provide stern warnings for those who embrace this mind-set.

Sadly, there are far too many masquerading as angels of light within the *body of Christ* who are reprobate.

The reprobates are an extreme example of how far down the wrong path some have gone. Beloved, I am charged with telling you the truth, so therefore, not everything I am writing will give you warm and fuzzy feelings. Nevertheless, it is the truth.

Simply stated, if you are one who is masquerading as an angle of light, there is another final warning I am charged with to share with you.

> *"Know ye not that the unrighteous shall not inherit the kingdom of God? Be not deceived: neither fornicators, nor idolaters, nor adulterers, nor effeminate, nor abusers of themselves with mankind, Nor thieves, nor covetous, nor drunkards, nor revilers, nor extortioners, shall inherit the kingdom of God"* (2 Cor. 6:9–11, KJV).

> *"And said, "Truly I say to you, unless you are converted and become like children, you will not enter the kingdom of heaven"* (Matt. 18:3, NASB).

> *"Not every one that saith unto me, Lord, Lord, shall enter into the kingdom of heaven; but he that doeth the will of my Father which is in heaven"* (Matt. 7:21, KJV).

So as you can see, if you are choosing to embrace any ungodly behaviors and have convinced yourself, *He* is fooled. Now is the time to confess your sins privately.

Also, I wanted you to be informed because if you have not already encountered church folks of this nature, you will.

The biblical explanations and spiritual discernment will enable you to recognize the manner of spirit you are dealing with at the onset, thus thwarting or avoiding chaos and confusion. Always be in prayer when you are accosted with people or church folks who embody the above characteristics. Pray for divine discernment and direction in order to be prepared.

On a lighter note, you will have ongoing doubts, and this is normal. However, if you apply the biblical principles listed in this chapter, you can overcome doubt.

On another front, if you do not apply biblical principles regarding dealing with doubt, lack of faith, and etc., you will be undermining peace in your life because there will be no basis of real security in your life, which can only come from *our Father in heaven* and *His* Word.

I have biblically covered all facets of doubt and the root cause within this chapter.

I would suggest read and reread the *Scriptures* with the intent to permanently apply into your way of thinking, thereby, beloved, removing the foothold of negative thinking within your psyche and giving way to know real peace.

Beloved, new uncharted horizons should be coming into clear view for you as I close this chapter.

I realize many pastors do not teach the above harsh realities, but they are charged to tell the truth, as I am.

You see, any sin tolerated, whether it is unbelief, doubt, or other sinful behaviors diminishes *His* ability to intervene for you.

In addition, if *the Father* tolerated any of our sin, it would mean *His* son *Jesus Christ* died for nothing. When you consider *Jesus Christ* died for all our sins, past, present, and future.

Beloved, I am not asking you to practice godly behaviors that I have not embraced because I have.

I know firsthand the beauty of submitting my very existence to the *Creator of the universe* for *His* divine purposes in my life. There is no greater joy!

There is no more toiling biblical gray areas, confusion, or chaos in my world. I have purposely adapted to *His* perfect will to be done in every facet of my life.

I am hopeful you will make the same decision today in order to breathe life into your world. Therefore, your choice to change the way you think about doubt and other sinful thinking patterns will open new doors of unimaginable horizons.

CHAPTER 6

Stay Focused

"Oh how I love your law day and night! It is my meditation all day" (Ps. 119:97, ESV).

When you are struggling with adjusting to your *deferred hope* status, it is extremely difficult to remain focused.

Simply stated, there are so many issues you are probably juggling at once. In most cases, dealing with numerous issues at one time is taxing on the human mind.

Many of us have noticeable limitations with managing stress properly. In addition to dealing with *deferred hope* and all the other issues this brings, managing stress levels can be a daunting task.

Human beings are not designed to handle enormous amounts of stress and pressures of this world. Think for a moment. Why do you think many of the hospital beds are always full? Do you believe any of the health issues are related to stress? It has been proven over and over again within the medical community that stress is the cause of many health issues.

Posted on the website www.webmd.com was an article featured by *Marie Claire* magazine entitled "What Stress Does to Your Body," written by Naomi Barr in 2008:

"The human body is well-adapted to deal with short-term stress, but if it remains on orange alert

for an extended period of time, you can grow vulnerable to some serious health problems."

This well-written article went on to state common health conditions caused by long-term stress—I am paraphrasing—such as the nervous system issues, endocrine problems, adrenal malfunctions, respiratory problems, cardiovascular, reproductive, weaken immune system, digestive issues, musculoskeletal problems, and the list goes on and on.

Many within our society internalize issues that cause stress in their lives, which can result in serious medical conditions. I used to be this way too until I realized my health could no longer afford to carry the weight of the world.

In the twenty-first century, the average individual that resides within the United States of America, who has a family, business owner, and is in the workforce, is dealing with stress. It does not matter, whether people admit to it or not, this is how many people live daily.

It matters not if the employees are the CEO, CFO, COO, CIO, IT director, manager, supervisor, administrative assistant, teacher, janitor, or the garbage disposer. All employment, or especially unemployment, brings a measure of stress to people. How did we get to this place, you ask?

When you think in terms of what could be the root causes of stress or lack of focus, there are many culprits.

No longer do many of us have the simple lifestyles that our parents and their parents enjoyed. Our parents and grandparents had stressors, but still, life was more simplistic.

Our daily lives are littered with stressful events, one after another. Actually, it is even more of a challenge to stay focused on what *His* Word says to us. Basically, I am saying to you, sin brings about stress, thus this thwarts focus.

"Trust in the LORD with all your heart; And do not lean on your own understanding.

> *In all your ways acknowledge Him, And He will make your paths straight"* (Prov. 3:5–6, NASB).

Just think, what if Adam and Eve had done this? Although the *New Testament* had not been written, they both knew what they were doing was wrong.

The origin of stress began with Adam and Eve. Before each one of them took a bite from the forbidden fruit in the Garden of Eve, they lived virtually stress-free lives. Adam and Eve had food supplied by God himself.

> *"And out of the ground made the LORD God to grow every tree that is pleasant to the sight, and good for food; the tree of life also in the midst of the garden, and the tree of knowledge of good and evil"* (Gen. 2:9, KJV).

But after Adam and Eve disobeyed *the Creator*, the ground became cursed, and they both had to work hard from that point forward. Their disobedient behavior was the beginning of the downfall for mankind until this day.

> *"And unto Adam he said, Because thou hast hearkened unto the voice of thy wife, and hast eaten of the tree, of which I commanded thee, saying, Thou shalt not eat of it: cursed is the ground for thy sake; in sorrow shalt thou eat of it all the days of thy life"* (Gen. 2:17, KJV).

> *"Thorns also and thistles shall it bring forth to thee; and thou shalt eat the herb of the field"* (Gen. 2:18, KJV).

> *"In the sweat of thy face shalt thou eat bread, till thou return unto the ground; for out of it wast thou*

taken: for dust thou art, and unto dust shalt thou return." (Gen. 2:19, KJV).

After the fall, Adam had to work the land by the sweat of his brow to provide food for himself and his family. Can you imagine the stress and lack of focus this caused for both of them?

Many of our ancestry lines lived by the golden rule of their day. The golden rule of the nineteenth and twentieth centuries was, "Do unto others as you would have them to you." Of course, as we all know the golden rule of this era gone by still applies to today (http://www.essex1.com/people/paul/bible-golden-rule.html).

It is unspoken but I believe *the Father* honored their mind-set.

Of course, in reality, it takes the power of the *Holy Spirit* and *His* Word to keep one focused while they are going through. This is the truth, pure and simple.

As you make time to pray and study *His* Word daily, divine help will be within view.

Many believers have untapped gifts, such as, teaching the Word to others, ministering, and missionary work, to name a few. The only thing is many are so focused on their problems that they neglect to utilize the spiritual gifts within.

One main component of remaining focused is to utilize your God-given talents while enduring deferred hope.

After years of one bad choice after the other, I finally found direction through prayer and supplication to pursue exactly what I wanted to do.

It was early March 2000. I had enrolled in DeVry Institute of Irving, Texas, to pursue a bachelor's degree in computer science.

I was so excited to finally be pursuing the degree I had longed to obtain so many years ago. And then a week or so after my enrollment into college, I called to Meridian, Mississippi, where my dad was staying with his sister. My father had elected to remain living with his sister after a major stroke several years earlier.

Well, as fate would have it, my dad's sister (Aunt Susie) had a major stroke, and she had been hospitalized for an entire week. I was perplexed as to why no one in the family had called to tell me about it, considering there was no one to take care of my father. Dad was totally dependent on Aunt Susie to provide twenty-four-hour care for him, which included, but was not limited to, cooking his meals, baths, giving him his medicines, and taking him to his doctor appointment visits. After discussing the critical matter with my husband, Vince, he supported my assessment to immediately go to Meridian and bring my dad to Texas.

There were other sidebar events happening at this time. I had started a new job within the information technology field, and I had only been employed for a month. Plus, I had graduated from technical college a few months prior to accepting the position.

So I thought I was well on my way to pursuing long-term goals I had set. The plan for me was, after my sons graduated high school and went to college, I would proceed with deferred goals.

Of course, this was not to be, at least not as I had planned, so after prayerfully arranging for my dad to reside at a nearby nursing home permanently, Vince and I headed to Meridian, Mississippi, to pick him up.

I must tell you, I regretfully made the decision to cancel the opportunity of attending DeVry Institute before making the trip to Meridian. Although I knew this was the right thing to do, it was very hard.

Because I knew it would be impossible for me to oversee the proper care of my father at the nursing home unless I quit college. In addition, I knew instinctively I would need to be available to closely monitor his care because it would require several visits a week.

There went my dream to pursue a computer science degree at that time.

As it turned out, I was my father's only caregiver besides the dedicated nursing home staff. For the first two years of Dad's stay at the nursing home, after work, I was at the nursing home five to six days a week.

As my dad's daughter, I felt internally compelled to make sure I did everything I could to make sure he was comfortable and to ensure all his needs were met.

The labor of love was very time-consuming and required my attention at any given time, apart from work and being a wife, a mother, a church member, and a Sunday schoolteacher.

I can tell you without question that utilizing my gift of teaching Sunday school was my divinely orchestrated saving grace. After a period of time, I became overwhelmed with all the responsibilities and fell into a depression of sorts.

Speaking of deferred hope, I am well acquainted with this status.

Did I share with you; how many management positions I turned down at the package delivery company prior to taking care of my dad?

I was concerned about raising my boys and being available for them as much as possible as a full-time working mom. I could not imagine taking a management position that would have pulled me away from them even more.

Well, looking back at my life, I can see where *The Father* used my gift of teaching the Bible and Sunday school to teach others and me too. You see, *The Word* was for me first; and then it was for the people I was teaching. At least, that is how I interpreted it.

Actually, many of the biblical stories or Sunday school lessons I was teaching, the parables or stories paralleled with my life. I was teaching from personal experience of real pain; and firsthand knowledge of *"deferred hope"*.

I can vividly recall many times, I would be teaching Sunday school to children, pre-teens or adults; and the tears would just flow from my eyes, freely. And, then I would share my "personal testimony" regarding many of my life-altering experiences.

So, you can see, how the *Holy Spirit (one of the three persons of the Trinity)* taught me and my Sunday school students for many years.

Yes, my hope was deferred; and yes, these were very difficult times for me.

Three years after I admitted my dad into the nursing home, I prayerfully sought the mind of *The Creator* for direction on re-entering college. Since my father was well integrated into nursing home life; and I was more at ease with things.

So, I enrolled in the Court Reporting Institute of Dallas, TX; to pursue a degree in court reporting. After all, court reporting had been an alternate choice to a degree in computer science. Plus, attending court reporting college would take on three years opposed to four years or more to complete.

I had been enrolled in court reporting college for two years, with only a year or so left to finish. I was writing one-hundred and twenty words per minute well and on my way to obtaining the required 225 words per minute speed to graduate. Learning to write at the sound of speech (in shorthand) was not an easy skill to master, but I did it.

And, then I began to realize our youngest son needed help with his school work in high school in order to obtain an acceptable GPA to graduate high school.

Now, as if I was not overwhelmed enough with all the above, my husband and I convinced our youngest son to move into our home. The truth of the matter was, our son was in the 9th grade; and we did not realize he was functioning at the 7th grade level.

This was not good, at all.

Of course, this was not acceptable to me or my husband. For the second time, I quit college again. Please keep in mind; I did not want to quit college again.

But, burning the midnight oil staying up many, many nights assisting my son with school projects; such as, writing essays, working on science projects or English writing assignments began to take its toll.

I was forced to face reality; I was no longer passing my speed tests to advance to the next writing speed in court reporting classes; i.e., 140 wpm, 160 wpm, 180 wpm, 200 wpm and the final speed of 225 wpm.

So in September 2005, I dropped out of college again.

Beloved, as you can see, I am intimately acquainted with your plight of deferred hope. Quitting college again did not feel good at all.

Regardless of how difficult things may become in your life, if you live on this side of heaven, there is hope in *Him*.

However, as you apply the *Scriptures* and live in obedience to *His* will, there is hope, and you will feel it.

Unfortunately, many of us lose hope too soon and return back to what we know. Of course, resuming past behaviors can be devastating and only cause more problems.

Going back to familiar things or sinful behaviors can and will lead to self-disillusionment or worse. Sometimes in our life journey, unexpected things happen to us to test our faith. Life's trials will expose any and all our spiritual weaknesses without question.

Remember, *"faith is substance hoped for and the evidence of things not seen" (Heb. 11:1; NASB).*

In essence, you cannot see how *our Father* is going to work out your issues, nor can you know if *He* is even going to intervene. You cannot know how long your "deferred hope" situation will last, but *He* challenges us to have faith. This is hard to endure for many.

When you feel yourself attempting to manipulate your circumstances to speed things up, so to speak, this is a sign you do not trust the Lord.

Beloved, I know this sound harsh, but this is not the intent. In our natural state, many of us desire to have our way, so we, consciously or unconsciously, do things to alter our circumstances. Whether you admit this or not, it is still true; however, it is to your advantage to examine yourself truthfully.

This is not good; however, many of us ignore the warning signs and proceed to direct our own paths to our own hurt. I will say, relying on your own intellect can actually add more issues to your *"deferred hope status"*.

There are many within Christendom that rely solely on their intellect to work out their *"deferred hope status."*

When the above occurs, these folks have chosen carnality over what the Word of God clearly teaches. Basically, the *body of Christ* is plagued with this type of believer.

> *"And I, brethren, could not speak unto you as unto spiritual, but as unto carnal or fleshly, even as unto babes in Christ" (1 Cor. 3:1, KJV).*

Some carnal believers are a threat to order, and these folks distort the original intent of the *Scriptures*. Unfortunately, the *body of Christ* overflows with carnal or fleshly believers who really believe they are living for the Christ. Some carnal or fleshly believers confuse an actual spiritual transformation or being born-again unto salvation with works within the church.

To interpret in simple terms, some people believe if they show up to church on time, attend church regularly, sing in the choir, attend Bible study, and so on, they are a being a good Christian. The aforementioned assessment could not be further from the truth because according to the *Scriptures*, "we Must Be born again through Christ Jesus."

> "*Jesus answered and said unto him, Verily, verily, I say unto thee, Except a man be born again, he cannot see the kingdom of God. That which is born of the flesh is flesh; and that which is born of the Spirit is spirit. Marvel not that I said unto thee, Ye must be born again*" (John 3:3–7, KJV).

When a person is born-again through *Jesus Christ* and has accepted *Him* as their personal savior, this should be the beginning of a spiritual transformation.

> "*And be not conformed to this world: but be ye transformed by the renewing of your mind, that ye may prove what is that good, and acceptable, and perfect, will of God*" (Rom. 12:2, KJV).

The spiritual transformation or renewing of one's mind will gradually happen over a period of time, which will continue until death. In addition, one must hunger after God's Word and *His* version of righteousness as if their very existence depends on it.

Usually, a born-again believer who desires change will utilize every biblical tool available to them. This will include, but is not limited to, confession of sin, daily individual spirit-led Bible study, and constantly being in prayer, seeking *His* divine guidance, and they will seek *His* divinely inspired Bible teachings from others *He* leads them to.

A born-again believer who desires to shed the desire to sin will seek to live *His* standard of righteousness and not their own. They will begin to despise sin in their lives and constantly ask *the Father* to reveal areas within their lives to eradicate sin.

These believers seek *real change* to the point they desire to minimize sin within every aspect of their world. Simply stated, this type of believer has a healthy fear of *our Creator*.

Therefore, this enables those who submit their will to *His* will, by default, to shed any notion of self-sufficiency.

You see, carnal or fleshly believers have little or no desire to change or to live by biblical principles completely. Many masquerade as angels of light, deceiving others and themselves.

> *"And no marvel; for Satan himself is transformed into an angel of light" (2 Cor. 11:14, KJV).*

Some even have the appearance of being born-again and believe they are living for *Him*. Sadly, this is one of the worst forms of self-deception.

> *"Having a form of godliness, but denying the power thereof: from such turn away" (2 Tim. 3:5, KJV).*

Not to mention, the folks on this side of the camp can wreak havoc among believers and the church itself.

This type of person comes in different forms. For instance, some appear saved or born-again, but have chosen to live out the Christian life intellectually.

And many folks have not accepted Jesus Christ as their savior but have deceived themselves into believing they have. There is much more to be said about this.

Beloved, those who have spiritually discerning spirits (*endowed with the Holy Spirit gift of discernment*) can and will allow you to see through the carnal-minded Christian.

Please consider, any believer who sins (including me) is biblically considered as being carnal. The purpose is not to embrace or stay this way.

> *"If we say we have no sin, we deceive ourselves, and the truth is not in us"* (1 John 1:8, KJV).

Beloved, you are not the only one who has tried to speed things up. I am guilty too. Please know each time I attempted to fix this or that on my own, the situation became even more difficult. I've had to learn the hard way.

This is why I am able to elaborate much on the subject matter; it is from experience and the "school of hard knocks." As my beloved mother used to say, "you will learn from the school of hard knocks," but you will learn.

Life is not friendly, nor does it offer solutions to assist you with the proper focus, so it is easy to lose focus on what *His* Word teaches us.

For born-again believers biblical principles are the only solutions to give us comfort during our times of deferred hope.

The things we are to do in times of trials and tribulations are to utilize divinely given *spiritual gifts* within the *body of Christ*. For those who are maturing and developing believers, there are numerous spiritual gifts divinely given by the direction of the *Holy Spirit*.

Please read below:

> *"Romans 12: gifts of exhortation, giving, leadership, mercy, prophecy, service (hospitality) and teaching.*
>
> *"1 Corinthians 12: gifts of administration, apostleship, discernment, faith, healing, helping, knowledge, miracles, prophecy, teaching, tongues, tongues interpretation, and wisdom.*
>
> *"Ephesians 4: gifts of apostleship, evangelism, pastoring, prophecy and teaching"* (Ministry Tools Resource Center; http://mintools.com/gifts-list.htm).

There will be many trials and tribulations throughout a believer's lifetime. Therefore, I believe in prayerfully utilizing your spiritual gifts and fulfilling *His* commission. In addition, you will be contributing to the cause of Christ while you wait and work on your "deferred hope" status.

With consideration to all the noises of life—and there are many noises in life—one has to endure many things, day in and day out, so it would be easy to blame life's circumstances. However, blame is never a good stance to take. Unnecessarily blaming others for any issues will only delay healing and progress. Sure there are people who cause you stress, but do not get stuck.

Sometimes, *our Father* divinely interrupts our lives to cause us to mature spiritually in order to make us better witnesses for *His* glory.

Many have the idea that all the things we go through in life should be about our comfort, but you should know, as a believer, this could not be further from the truth. *The Father* will not sacrifice *His* glory for your comfort.

He is not concerned if you are comfortable with what *He* is doing in your life. Again, *He* cares about your life, and my life, giving *Him* absolute glory void of hypocrisy.

Beloved, pray to stay focused on what you were born to do. Give *the Creator of the universe* undivided allegiance, irrespective of your "deferred hope status".

CHAPTER 7

Obtain Godly Counsel

> *"Where there is no counsel, the people fall; But in the multitude of counselors there is safety". (Prov. 7:11, NKJV)*

I will point out to you that the first choice in determining what God is doing would be to seek Him in prayer and seek Him through His Word. The divinely inspired *Scriptures* will give you great insight on seeking wise counsel.

> *"The way of a fool is right in his own eyes: but he that hearkeneth unto counsel is wise" (Prov. 12:15, KJV).*

> *"Without counsel purposes are disappointed: but in the multitude of counsellors they are established" (Prov. 15:22, KJV).*

Let's reason for a moment, after studying and pondering the aforementioned *scriptures*, why do Christians seek counsel outside of what God's Word commands us to do?

I am guilty of not following *the Father's Word* for seeking wise counsel in my early years of being a Christian. Lack of belief and faith in *the Creator's* Word is the main reason many of us have gone outside *His* best for us.

I will admit to you, for many years, I thought it was God's Word, plus human wisdom, that would be my saving grace. However, I learned from trial and error that it is only *His* Word and *His* divine guidance and nothing else that would save me from myself. He always had a "ram in the bush" to assist me by placing godly mentors or counselors.

When believers do not follow *the Father's* godly wisdom regarding seeking wise counsel, there are always consequences.

I will never forget how I had confused the difference between a real Christian and a religious churchgoer. I learned this lesson the hard way. There is a difference. I was under the delusion that if a person attends church every Sunday and attended Bible study weekly, they were a born-again believer.

I had confided in a "religious churchgoer" unknowingly about personal issues I was experiencing. These folks can wreak havoc among the church body in a stealth-like manner. It was not long after confiding in private with this individual that other people within the church body were inquiring about my personal issue. Keep in mind, no one else was supposed to know! I was so embarrassed beyond what I can say because everyone knew about it!

I will not get into the issue, but clearly my personal issue is not the point. This was all about principles. You see, what I learned is, you cannot trust people because they attend church every Sunday.

The person you choose to trust for godly advice should be a born-again believer baptized with the *Holy Spirit*. It is then and only then that you should trust someone with any of your personal issues.

Simply stated, because a true born-again believer is accountable to God, and he or she understands their accountability to *the Creator*.

Therefore, this type of believer will not offend God due to what is at stake.

I touch on a couple of really serious reasons why believers should not disobey these life-saving *scriptures*. I have found over the years that many of our answers to life questions are within the *Scriptures*. This is not a cliché response; it is a true statement.

Studying God's Word diligently and praying and seeking *His* wisdom are not to be taken lightly. *Our Father in heaven* desires us to consult *Him* as our first choice. Now *He* will allow each of us to seek godly wisdom, to obtain human guidance, but there is always a limitation. However, it is a more excellent choice to seek *His* divine wisdom at the onset.

There are many examples within the Bible where God permitted judges to disseminate *His* divine wisdom.

For instance, within the book of Judges, Judges 3:7–11, there were several major judges who God had raised up to give godly counsel to the Israelites.

With God raising up judges to direct *His* chosen people (the Israelites), *He* demonstrated *His* omnipotent compassion toward them.

Sidebar note, according to *Biblical Law vs. the United States Constitution* by Ted Weiland (2002), it is believed by some biblical scholars that the book of Judges was the beginning of judicial systems all over the world (http://www.missiontoisrael.org/biblelaw-constitutionalism-pt6.php).

Let's think for a moment. God was and still is the ultimate judge of all the earth and its inhabitants.

God did not have to raise up judges to disseminate *His* divine wisdom. Surely, it was *His* compassion for *His* chosen children that caused *Him* to do this.

Be mindful, the Israelites were not under grace yet because the *Old Testament* times was BC or before Christ. Jesus had not come on to the scene yet.

The Israelites were under Judaism law, which they failed miserably.

The next question you may be asking is, what is Judaism?

According to *Dictionary.com*, the definition of *Judaism* is this:

> *"The monotheistic religion of the Jews, having its ethical, ceremonial, and legal foundation in the precepts of the Old Testament and in the teachings and commentaries of the rabbis as found chiefly in the Talmud. Compare Conservative Jew, Orthodox Jew, Reform Jew."*

Simply stated, Judaism was the law. Please know, if I had lived in those days, I would have failed the law much worse.

And after Moses was sent by God to save the Israelites from slavery in Egypt, God commanded Moses to give the Israelites—the *Ten Commandments* or the five Books of Moses or the Pentateuch.

> *"And the* LORD *said unto Moses, Come up to me into the mount, and be there: and I will give thee tables of stone, and a law, and commandments which I have written; that thou mayest teach them" (Exod. 24:12, KJV).*

The *Book of the Law* within the *Old Testament* was considered the first five Books of Moses or the Pentateuch. Also, the Book of Moses is referred to as *the Torah*.

The five *Books of Moses* are as follows: Genesis, Exodus, Leviticus, Numbers, and Deuteronomy.

The Father loved them so much, *He* raised up judges and kings to guide *His* people.

To learn more about *His* graciousness toward the Israelites, please study at your leisure 1 and 2 Samuel, 1 and 2 Kings, 1 and 2 Chronicles, and the book of Judges. These are rich books containing the history of the kings and how some followed God or some did not.

For instance, God raised up Othniel, who was the son of Caleb (Judg. 3:7–11), Ehud (Judg. 3:12–30), Jephthah (Judg. 11:1—12:7), Gideon (Judg. 6:11–8:35), Samson (Judg. 13:1–16:31), and Deborah (Judg. 4:1–5:31).

These were chosen judges that *He* raised up to advise the Israelites with their daily sin struggles.

Fast-forward to the twenty-first century. God still calls certain people of *His* choosing to minister and counsel *His* people. I am referring to those who are Gentiles (not Jewish) known as born-again Christians. However, I will stress to those who prefer counseling, please be sure the counselor you choose provide biblically based counseling. Seeking godly counseling is absolutely critical to finding balance and a biblically based understanding. Actually, many in our progressive society choose secular-minded counselors. Unfortunately, many of secular-minded counselors do not adhere to godly principles; therefore, the advice given is usually from a worldly prospective.

A counselor guided by the direction of the *Holy Spirit* will lead you back to the *Scriptures* without fail because he or she clearly understands they are accountable to *the Creator* regarding the instructions provided.

As a matter of fact, I will go so far to say that anyone that is under the divine guidance of *the God of the Bible* must provide biblically inspired counseling or they will be held accountable too.

Godly counselors will point you to *scriptures* that will give you hope during your "deferred hope" status.

There are countless secular counselors available at the click of a mouse button. I will warn you, obtaining counseling from a secular prospective or from a fleshly standpoint could be disastrous for a believer.

On this side of the fence, secular-minded counselors have no interest in counseling the masses according to God's Word. In many cases, this camp completely reject a biblical prospective of counseling.

Let me just say this, born-again Christians should *never* seek secular-minded counselors for wise counsel.

When I was a child, I can still remember many of the "old folks" who professed to be Christians went to obtain counseling from fortune-tellers.

I have to admit I did not understand why many of their lives were in such chaos until I became older. I certainly gained a biblical understanding of what had happened to them.

Unfortunately for them who had taken this destructive path, they did not trust God as their savior. The sad part is many of them attended church every Sunday but did not believe in Jesus.

You see, the *Scriptures* are clear: God's elect are not supposed to seek soothsayers or fortune-tellers for counsel.

> *"'As for the person who turns to mediums and to spiritists, to play the harlot after them, I will also set My face against that person and will cut him off from among his people" (Lev 20:6).*

The Father has not changed *His* mind about what *His* Word states we are to do.

Read the *scriptures* below from the *Old Testament* regarding Manasseh's and Saul's stories.

He (Manasseh) practiced divination and magic and *consulted fortune-tellers and mediums.* He *sinned greatly* against the Lord and stirred up his *anger* (2 Kings 21.6; 2 Chron. 33:6). Read also 1 Samuel 28:3–25.

> *"And he [Manasseh] set a graven image of the grove that he had made in the house, of which the* Lord *said to David, and to Solomon his son, In this house, and in Jerusalem, which I have chosen out of all tribes of Israel, will I put my name for ever" (2 Kings 21:7, KJV).*

Saul, the king (God chose him), to be installed by Samuel had the "*Spirit of God*" to leave him, so he consulted a medium toward his end.

> *"Now Samuel was dead, and all Israel had mourned for him and buried him in his own town of Ramah. Saul had expelled the mediums and spiritists from the land.*
>
> *"The Philistines assembled and came and set up camp at Shunem, while Saul gathered all Israel and set up camp at Gilboa. When Saul saw the Philistine army, he was afraid; terror filled his heart. He inquired of the* Lord, *but the* Lord *did not answer him by dreams or Urim or prophets. Saul*

> *then said to his attendants, "Find me a woman who is a medium, so I may go and inquire of her.*
>
> *"'There is one in Endor,' they said.*
>
> *"So Saul disguised himself, putting on other clothes, and at night he and two men went to the woman. 'Consult a spirit for me,' he said, 'and bring up for me the one I name.'*
>
> *"But the woman said to him, 'Surely you know what Saul has done. He has cut off the mediums and spiritists from the land. Why have you set a trap for my life to bring about my death?'*
>
> *"Saul swore to her by the* LORD, *'As surely as the* LORD *lives, you will not be punished for this.'*
>
> *"Then the woman asked, 'Whom shall I bring up for you?'*
>
> *"'Bring up Samuel,' he said" (1 Sam. 28:3–11).*

Beloved, do you think *the Father* would be happy if you and I consulted these folks? Regardless of the issue(s), if believers seek counseling of any kind, it will be beneficial to seek a counselor who embraces God's biblical point of view.

So while you are in your spiritual quest to obtain an understanding of your "deferred hope status", there is the option of seeking godly counseling.

By seeking godly wisdom, you avoid falling into sin, thus avoiding more problems for yourself. Your enemy, the devil, is just waiting for you to make the wrong choice.

> *"And the* LORD *said unto Satan, Whence comest thou? Then Satan answered the* LORD, *and said, From going to and fro in the earth, and from walking up and down in it" (Job 1:7, KJV).*

> *"Be sober, be vigilant; because your adversary the devil, as a roaring lion, walketh about, seeking whom he may devour" (1 Pet. 5:8, KJV).*

The enemy (*the devil*) desires to destroy your testimony, and even your life, if he can, so please precede with extreme caution.

Many within the *body of Christ* turn to close relatives or a trusted friend to assist them during this lengthy process. Beloved, you still should be very careful with confiding and consulting with friends or family too. If you feel, you must talk it out with someone, please be prayerful in allowing the *Holy Spirit* to direct you to a trustworthy, God-led confidant. I make this statement because the above application applies to friends and relatives too.

All too often, if the advice or counseling your relatives or friends provide is not biblically based, you could be headed for disaster. Unfortunately, many of our relatives, friends, and churchgoing acquaintances are not as well-versed and grounded in the *Scriptures* as they appear to be. To interpret, the *Word of God* must be sealed into their hearts.

Then there is the issue of confiding in someone that you think is a trusted confidant. And this individual betrays your trust by divulging your personal information to others, therefore not only betraying your trust but also sharing potentially damaging personal information. I know that sometime in your life, this has happened to you. This happened to me, as I discussed earlier. For me, it took years to repair the damage done by so-called Christians. We all endured at some point in time, the damage done by a trusted confidant; the damage was irreparable. Therefore, this caused valued relationships to be destroyed.

Is this not what the devil desires? To have relationships permanently destroyed? Satan's main objective is to sow seeds of despair throughout the *body of Christ*.

As I stated above, I have had to learn the hard way, because some people who say they are Christians are not always what they seem.

The *Scriptures* give us the guidance we need for testing people to see if they are; who they say they are. This is extremely critical for a believer seeking wise counsel. However, in order to test what manner of person you are dealing with, you must be spiritually discerning yourself, or you can and will be deceived by the enemy.

> *"Beloved, believe not every spirit, but try the spirits whether they are of God: because many false prophets are gone out into the world"* (1 John 4:1, KJV).

The *body of Christ* is filled with so-called believers masquerading as angels of light.

> *"And no wonder, for Satan himself masquerades as an angel of light"* (2 Cor. 11:14, NASB).

Beloved, I know this is hard to absorb and to believe, but it is the truth!

I have had personal experiences over the years with people who represented themselves as Christians, but their focus was to destroy me, directly or indirectly. Hopefully, you are already aware this sort of thing exists within the *body of Christ*.

I am of the opinion (and this is just my opinion) that the closer we get to the Rapture, the more Satan is integrating his minions within the *body of Christ*.

> *"For the Lord himself shall descend from heaven with a shout, with the voice of the archangel, and with the trump of God: and the dead in Christ shall rise first: Then we which are alive and remain shall be caught up together with them in the clouds, to meet the Lord in the air: and so shall we ever be with the Lord"* (1 Thess. 4:16–17, KJV).

The above *scriptures* are considered *the Rapture* of *the Father's* elect.

As defined by *Merriam-Webster's* online dictionary, *rapture* means "the final assumption of Christians into heaven during the end-time according to Christian theology."

The Rapture will occur right before the Tribulation period, also known as the judgment period. This is foretold in the book of Revelation.

> *"Because thou hast kept the word of my patience, I also will keep thee from the hour of temptation, which shall come upon all the world, to try them that dwell upon the earth. Behold, I come quickly: hold that fast which thou hast, that no man take thy crown"* (Rev. 3:10–11, KJV).

I believe Satan's efforts, for the most part, have been successful. I make this statement because if you look at our nation in its entirety, the church, in particular, has lost its power in the culture.

No longer do people respect the church. The church used to be the bedrock of our national society—or the social conscience of our nation, if you will.

Now it is quite normal to hear on any national or local news media outlets that there has been a shooting or a robbery at a church sanctuary or worse.

These types of things happening at church used to be nonexistent in the twentieth century, but now this sort of thing is commonplace in the twenty-first century. Does it seem to you that the church is no longer respected or seen as a viable conscious conduit for our nation? This cannot be a good thing for our nation. Of course, as you well know, there are many more unmentionable things happening within the United States and other nations that grieve *the Holy Spirit*.

According to *Dictionary.com*, the definitions of the word *grieve* is "to feel great sorrow; or to distress mentally."

Going forward, to make the issue of seeking ungodly counsel concrete to you, when a believer seeks ungodly counsel, this too grieves the Holy Spirit:

> *"And grieve not the Holy Spirit of God, by whom you are sealed unto the day of redemption"* (Eph. 4:30, KJV).

Beloved, for a biblical understanding of this point, clearly you should understand that doing anything outside of what the *Scriptures* command you to do *will grieve the Holy Spirit*. Surely, you can see why seeking godly counseling is critical to your growth and spiritual development as a believer.

I am sharing all this information from the standpoint of years of biblical studying, application, and experience.

Beloved, if today, you make the choice to integrate these priceless truths into your heart and mind, you will avoid a lot of heartache and delay. On another front, if you have made the mistake I did in the past, seeking counseling from other resources, there is still hope.

First, I would suggest asking *the Father* to forgive you for your error in judgment.

Second, going forward, seek only *Holy Spirit*-led counsel.

I am not saying if you do all the above that *the Father* will reveal to you why your "hope has been deferred." After all, *He* is God, and *He* has the last say on all your life circumstances. I have merely provided biblical references to encourage you to seek *His* way as opposed to your own way.

Because as you have learned, seeking counseling your way will lead to failure and heartache.

Last—and I know this is a rhetorical question but I am posing it to provoke thought—will you continue do things your way?

CHAPTER 8

Embrace the Revelations Gained

"Do you want to unfailingly go with Christ in the rapture of the saints or go to heaven when you die? Examine yourself by the revelations of this book and have a proper vision of heaven and the life that qualifies for it" (Michael Thomas Sambo).

In your quest to determine the reason(s) for your *deferred hope status*, be sure to expose yourself to all potential help discussed within the previous chapter.

The revelations revealed to you from spending quality time studying the *Scriptures* are a major accomplishment. I will even step out and say, continue to study the *Scriptures* because *His* words will provide ongoing comfort to you. It does not matter what you are going through in life, as time goes on, the Bible continues to be a source of comfort. Sure, there are other sources of comfort, but I am of the opinion there is none better than the divinely inspired *Word of God*.

The other sources of comfort I am referring to are friends, associates, or family members. Many of us choose these sources of comfort naturally, without thinking, but there is no better comfort than seeking divine comfort from the *Scriptures* or *the Creator Himself*. Please take time to sort out what *our Father* has revealed to you through the direction of the *Holy Spirit*.

If you have devoted quality time studying the *Scriptures* and prayer and it is *our Father's* perfect will, then *He* may reveal why you are in "deferred hope status".

It is never too late to do the above—never.

But there is the possibility *He* may not reveal anything to you regarding your circumstances. Are you still going to be faithful although you have not heard from God? Are you still going to trust *His* divine guidance and direction? Remember, to be patient and long-suffering because this could and will take time. You see, God is God!

Let's consider Job, one of God's faithful servants. Job was known throughout the land as a blameless and upright man who feared God and avoided evil.

> *"There was a man in the land of Uz, whose name was Job; and that man was perfect and upright, and one that feared God, and eschewed evil"* (Job 1:1, KJV).

Although Job was living in Old Testament times, which was considered still *under the law or before Christ, BC*, he still knew and understood his commitment to God. Job was obedient and faithful. This was one of the many stories left behind for us in the Bible to exact obedience, regardless of circumstances.

Many within Christendom desire all their trials and tribulations to be pleasant and nonthreatening. This is not real Christianity by any means.

Real Christianity is marred with suffering and being ostracized from society. In many countries outside of the United States, Christians are tortured and persecuted.

Sure, there are various forms of persecution from secular institutions within these United States. For instance, at all American schools prayers to the *God of the Bible* or *Jesus Christ* are not permitted.

The ultimate rejection of *Jesus Christ* for America is when prayer was banned from public schools by the United States Supreme Court in 1962.

Madalyn O'hair spearheaded a federal lawsuit that led to her personal ideas of separation of church and state being implemented as the law of the land (http://www.allaboutpopularissues.org/prayer-in-the-public-schools-faq.htm).   I brought up the above issues to clearly point out an example of Job's obedience within the *Old Testament*. I can tell you from experience, *obedience is better than sacrifice* to those who submit to *His* will.

> *"And Samuel said, Hath the LORD as great delight in burnt offerings and sacrifices, as in obeying the voice of the LORD? Behold, to obey is better than sacrifice, and to hearken than the fat of rams"* (1 Sam. 15:22, KJV).

I know this is not an easy thing to do at the onset. I have personally attempted to go around God's perfect design for my life, but I suffered the consequences.

Many years ago, I received revelations directly from the *scripture*. While studying the Bible under the direction of the *Holy Spirit* (my faithful teacher), I began to see why my *hope was deferred*.

It was revealed to me scripturally that my own sinful choices were the cause of my *"hope deferred status"*. Now, I grant you, this was not an easy revelation to absorb.

After all, I knew what I was doing, right? In my own humanness, I thought the choices I was making would somehow cause a good outcome in my life.

Well, my prideful and arrogant assessment could not have been further from the truth.

> *"Pride goes before destruction, And a haughty spirit before stumbling"* (Prov. 16:18, NASB).

And, oh boy, did I fall and stumble for many, many years.

You see, self-deception is one of the worst forms of denial an individual can possess. Unfortunately, within the *body of Christ*, this is quite prevalent.

Since I have lived a life of self-deception, I am familiar with how it looks and what it sounds like. This is why a believer cannot trust their *own heart* or mind—because we are all naturally wicked and deceitful.

I know the secular point of view suggests we should trust "our heart" when making life decisions, but this will have you living in complete error.

> *"The heart is deceitful above all things, and desperately wicked: who can know it"* (Jer. 17:9).

So can you really trust your heart as the secular world suggests?

He decides and *He* alone chooses whether or not to reveal things to us. *Our Father* is not like man that *He* can be manipulated by humans.

Some believers believe if they do all the aforementioned, *our Father* will yield to what they want *Him* to do. This is not true.

Our Father does not cater at will for us unless *He* has a divine purpose for intervening in certain matters. Many times over, *He* does not reveal to us what *He* is up to.

He is God, and *He* governs what to reveal as *He* chooses. It is our responsibility as believers to trust *Him* regardless.

This will not be easy to do, but it is necessary to remain in obedience.

In cases such as this, *the Father* expects us to embrace *His* work in blind faith.

Remember, *"faith is the substance of things hoped for and the evidence of things not seen"* (Heb. 11:1, KJV).

Basically, you have to submit your will to *our Father's* divine wisdom and guidance even if *He* has not answered. This is not easy to do, but you must do it. *Our Father* only honors obedience contrary to what many choose to believe.

Let's say, for example, *the Father* reveals to you from a godly counselor why your *hope has been deferred*. This is with consideration; the counselor and the counseling are biblically connected.

When and if you are given a reason why hope is deferred you will be blessed.

This is not always the case.

The next thing to do is to apply what *He* has revealed to your life circumstances immediately. Do not hesitate to yield to divine wisdom, as this will benefit you greatly. Plus, you will be stronger in having faith going forward.

Because when *He* responds to and answers your inquiries, this builds incredible faith. Even in situations of this nature, *our Father* demonstrates patience and grace toward us.

You see, *our Father* knows we have limitations as human beings; after all, *He* created us.

Beloved, respect and appreciate your trials regardless how big or small because tribulations build patience and godly character like nothing else I know.

Has it occurred to you that everything you have suffered through up unto this point was meant to be? I am hopeful that you are beginning to understand that trials and tribulations are a huge part of your Christian walk.

It is not easy being a born-again Christian. I know many pastors and church congregations buy into the heresy that becoming a Christian is easy. It is not.

Sidebar, I've witnessed ministers and pastors teaching in error, "All you have to do is accept Jesus, and your troubles will be over."

Quite the contrary, when you make a commitment to live out the Christian life obediently, *all hell breaks loose*. As a matter of fact, you should expect to receive opposition from every facet of your life, including, but not limited to, your immediate family, relatives, friends, church members (*yes, I said church members*), and coworkers.

In order to make it through the endless trials, a true believer must be deeply rooted in the *Scriptures* and *prayer*.

Beloved, also you must constantly nurture your spiritual relationship with *the Father*. Apart from your growing relationship with *the Father*, the aforementioned suggestions are absolutely critical to your contentment.

This will be very hard on you, and, yes, you will have setbacks due to your frail human state.

Beloved, we have so many limitations as human beings. You cannot trust your own thoughts or your own opinions. If so, this will lead you down another disastrous road of disappointment.

I cannot stress to you enough to put into daily practice the divine revelations that were revealed to you. I would like to share with you a few major reasons why this is so critical to your walk with *the Father*.

The reasons I listed is not a limited list.

First, reason it is vitally important for you submit to wise counsel is this will cause you to grow spiritually.

Second, reason is your faith will become fortified due to "complete trust in *His* divine guidance and direction."

Third, you will no longer fear opposition or be hindered spiritually by your "*deferred hope status*". You will flourish.

Last but not least, you will encourage others directly or indirectly while you are "in transition."

And the last reason is huge, to say the least.

When people in general inquire about the *hope that is within you*, this could be an incredible moment to witness. As the *Holy Spirit* guides your thought process during this critical appointment, let *Him* use you to bring the lost to Christ.

> "*But sanctify the Lord God in your hearts: and be ready always to give an answer to every man that asketh you a reason of the hope that is in you with meekness and fear*" (1 Pet. 3:15, KJV).

There is the opposite side of the fence to consider.

You could also potentially cause other believers to stumble because you have chosen not to take the circumstances seriously enough. This is a spiritual matter.

What do I mean by saying this? I am so glad you asked.

It is wrong to believe that all that you are going through is *only about you*. This assessment could not be further from the truth.

Many self-centered believers have chosen this path only to cause many to stumble in the faith. Please know you will not be blameless in this matter.

> *"That ye may be blameless and harmless, the sons of God, without rebuke, in the midst of a crooked and perverse nation, among whom ye shine as lights in the world" (Phil. 2:15, KJV).*

It is true, believers are supposed to be following Christ as the ultimate example for Christianity. We should live in such a way that reflects who Christ is by how we live and not bring reproach to ourselves. According to the *Scriptures*, we are to avoid any appearance of evil.

> *"Abstain from all appearance of evil" (1 Thess. 5:22, KJV).*

The Father will hold you accountable because not only is *His* glory at stake, but so are souls. Whenever an individual falls deeper into sin because of your careless actions, there will be consequences. I cannot tell you what the consequences will be because this is *the Father's* business, not mine.

The following *scripture* is clear:

> *"For it had been better for them not to have known the way of righteousness, than, after they have known it, to turn from the holy commandment delivered unto them" (2 Pet. 2:21, KJV).*

As you faithfully embrace and walk in your biblical revelations, you will encourage nonbelievers to believe on *Him* just by your walk.

Have you ever heard of the old saying, "You may be the only Jesus some people will see"?

This is an old adage, but in many cases, it is a true statement.

As our society becomes more godless and unholy, it is not far-fetched to believe the above statement. As a matter of fact, it is becoming more common for many within the *body of Christ* to reject biblical standards instead of secular society. Yes, I said it. Unfortunately, for Christendom, the congregations are moving more toward secularism than biblical standards. Anyone who professes to be a believer cannot afford to underestimate the power of their realm of influence to others.

Beloved, you can see why it is absolutely critical for you to walk in *Him* during this lengthy process. There will always be ongoing challenges for you to deal with, but keep in mind who *the author and finisher of your faith is*.

> *"Looking unto Jesus the author and finisher of our faith; who for the joy that was set before him endured the cross, despising the shame, and is set down at the right hand of the throne of God"* (Heb. 12:2, KJV).

If you completely trust *Him*, there will always be help through *His* Word, prayer, church messages, and fellow believers.

I have clear and convincing biblical references for why it is imperative to embrace the revelations revealed to you. Please take time to study the *Scriptures* at your leisure. In addition to studying the *Scriptures*, it is even more crucial for you to apply the biblical principles to your life.

As I grew in grace (an understanding of the biblical interpretation of Scriptures), I made a conscious decision to apply all that I was learning to my daily life.

> *"Wisdom is the principal thing; therefore get wisdom: and with all thy getting get understanding"* (Prov. 4:7, KJV).

You see, as I studied the *Scriptures*, I believed *the Father* was speaking to me personally, through *His* Word.

I felt, and I still believe, that the Bible serves as a mirror reflecting its light into my life. Thus, the truths I read cause me to make a decision immediately.

What will I do about what I have studied?

I have chosen to apply, and still choose to apply, biblical principles into my life. I believe this is one of the most important decisions, besides accepting Christ as my personal savior.

By consciously deciding to *be more like Christ, the Father* has honored my spiritual growth beyond anything I could have ever imagined.

Basically, I did what I am suggesting for you to do.

I studied the Bible (daily, and I still do). I apply and live what I learn, and I *pray without ceasing* (1 Thess. 5:17).

To be hearers of the Word and not doers of the Word is considered sin, according to the *Scriptures*. See below.

> "But be ye doers of the word, and not hearers only, deceiving your own selves" (James 1:22, KJV).

You see, I believe this to be true, and I adjust, accordingly.

Beloved, until the biblical *Rapture* occurs spoken of, in 1 Thessalonians, I will study and apply *scriptures*, attend church, witness, and serve the Cause of Christ.

> "Then we which are alive and remain shall be caught up together with them in the clouds, to meet the Lord in the air: and so shall we ever be with the Lord" (1 Thess. 4:17, KJV).

I desire to be caught in well-doing, when *He* comes to remove the church from society.

> "And let us not be weary in well doing: for in due season we shall reap, if we faint not" (Gal. 6:9, KJV).

Beloved, as you can see, this is serious business.

I am saddened and disappointed when I see believers not giving in to the weight of what the *Scriptures* command. There is no place within the Bible where *the Father* suggested any of the *scriptures* is multiple choice.

In other words, you cannot choose the sections you are in agreement with and discard the chapters that you do not agree with. As ridiculous as this might sound, this is exactly what is happening in Christendom in the twenty-first century.

Beloved, please know that going forward, as you make decisions that will give *our Creator* the ultimate glory, you will meet opposition. As a matter of fact, be prepared for complete resistance in your sphere of influence and beyond. You will become acquainted with rejection from family members, church members, friends, acquaintances, and in every facet of your life because, keep in mind, there are a lot of people in the church body who are *playing church*. Many people in this crowd has pretty much nailed down how to be religious and have the appearance of being saved to a fine art.

Note, being endowed with the gift of discernment, *The Holy Spirit* will reveal to you who they are.

> "*To another the working of miracles; to another prophecy;* **to another discerning of spirits;** *to another divers kinds of tongues; to another the interpretation of tongues*: 1 Corinthians 12:10 KJV[175]

> "*In latter days, deceitful spirits and doctrines of demons will come, so the important role of the gift of discernment is to identify those spirits and doctrines*". 1Timothy 4:1 KJV[176]

These folks are within the *Body of Christ*, so beware, because you will be persecuted.

Do not be discouraged, because the saints of old had to deal with the deceitful spirits, as well.

"Blessed are they which are persecuted for righteousness' sake: for theirs is the kingdom of heaven". Matthew 5:10 KJV[177]

"Blessed are ye, when men shall revile you, and persecute you, and shall say all manner of evil against you falsely, for my sake". Matthew 5:11 KJV[177]

Beloved, I will add to the above assessment; and say "if you are not being persecuted; you probably look too much like the world". You are not a threat to the establishment.

Maybe your Christian walk is of non-effect; and non-challenging, to those in your sphere of influence.

I am not writing this book to make you feel comfortable. I wrote this book to challenge those who claim to be a Christian *"to walk in it"*.

To void you of hypocrisy, as so many do in Christendom; and substitute practicing hypocrisy, as biblical principles.

The world must be able see; and test your true embracement of the revelations gained.

Adjust and be blessed!

CHAPTER 9

Was the Suffering Worth It?

"And after you have suffered a little while, the God of all grace, who has called you to his eternal glory in Christ, will himself restore, confirm, strengthen, and establish you" (1 Pet. 5:10, ESV).

Responding to the question put forth, was the suffering worth it? This question will yield different answers from believers.

A believer's response depends largely on how each person has yielded to their *"deferred hope status."* In addition to this, it also depends whether the believer is maturing or is biblically growing in grace. To put it simply, where you are in your Christian walk depends on how you will answer the question above.

Jesus Christ died on the cross for our past, present, and future sins.

And before Jesus was hung on the cross at Golgotha, *He* suffered tremendously. Many times, Golgotha (or place of the skull) is referred to as Calvary by modern-day pastors (John 19:17).

It stands to human reason, if Jesus suffered, those who embrace Christianity are going to suffer too. My comfort in suffering is this: *"Your promise preserves my life"* (Ps. 119:50, NIV).

A mature believer accepts his or her divinely orchestrated circumstances. However, I will not mislead you into thinking this will not be a painful process because it will be. In addition, a mature believer views suffering as not only being worth it but also a part of their divine calling to live out their servanthood life.

In spite of what you hear via the media and other communication mediums, living out the Christian life is not easy. Living out the Christian life is a daily commitment and surrender to *our Creator* to glorify *Him*.

Growing in grace means a believer is maturing biblically by developing a godly understanding of God's Word and application.

For a believer who has accepted his or her *"deferred hope status"* is a person whose will is completely submitted to *our Father's* divine directives in their lives. This individual avidly studies God's Word and seeks *His* mind on a daily basis, in addition to "praying without ceasing" (1 Thess. 5:17, NASB).

This person seeks ways to serve others while they are in their *"deferred hope status"*. Regardless of our human circumstances or condition as believers, we are still *His* servants.

Did Jesus not set the example for us to follow?

If a believer is servitude-minded, they will be drawn to serve others as the *Holy Spirit* leads them.

A person with this level of maturity realizes whether or not *the Father* answers their inquiries or not, it is imperative they remain obedient and honor *Him*.

Are you at this point yet?

On another front, a believer who is not maturing spiritually will be resistant to submission. Actually, a believer who resists being a servant is considered carnal. According to the *Scriptures*, *"Because the carnal mind is enmity against God: for it is not subject to the law of God, neither indeed can be"* (Rom. 8:7, KJV).

The *Scriptures* are clear about a believer choosing to remain carnal-minded. Many choose not to grow biblically, or they choose by default not to grow. Not choosing is the same thing as choosing. When a believer is carnal-minded, it is impossible for them to grow spiritually. This embodied behavior grieves the *Holy Spirit*, thus hindering *His* ability to help them.

"And grieve not the holy Spirit of God, whereby ye are sealed unto the day of redemption" (Eph. 4:30, KJV).

Grieving (or making sad) the *Holy Spirit* is sinful and will cause a continuance of error and other missteps.

This individual is full of their own opinions as opposed to being full of the *Holy Spirit*, who could really help them grow.

Beloved, be careful not to take the destructive route discussed above.

I am hopeful this book has caused you to reconsider the direction you have been traveling.

I believe many Christians attempt to live the Christian life through their own strength and human insight. Living the Christian life without the help of *the Father* and our teacher, the *Holy Spirit*, is impossible.

One thing I have made clear is this: you will suffer, and you will not be liked in many circles.

But this is okay.

I discussed in the previous chapter 8 that you will be persecuted. This is what happens to real Christians. You see, believers who are walking the walk thoroughly understand he or she will be tormented and ostracized.

In my opinion, Christians who reside in the United States cannot fully appreciate the freedom of witnessing until their exposed to what happens in other countries. In the United States, we enjoy freedom of speech under the *First Amendment of the United States Constitution*, passed in 1791.

The First Amendment to the US Constitution reads,

> *"Congress shall make no law respecting an establishment of religion, or prohibiting the free exercise thereof; or abridging the freedom of speech, or of the press; or the right of the people peaceably to assemble, and to petition the Government for a redress*

of grievances" (http://constitution.findlaw.com/ amendment1/amendment.html).

Therefore, the above constitutional law gives every American federal protection under the freedom of speech, namely, the First Amendment.

Americans are protected under the law to discuss Christianity freely, at the time of the writing of this book. I make this statement because it appears the tide is beginning to shift drastically. More and more, the right to free speech within America is being challenged as high as the Supreme Court level.

Since my book is not about free speech, I elect to move on. I merely wanted to point out how blessed our nation is to have the ability to speak freely about Christianity.

In America, we do not have to be concerned about being tortured or martyred. So with that being said, we should use every opportunity to witness our faith to a dying world.

To intellectual minds, embracing suffering seems to be outlandish and appears totally ludicrous, to say the very least, but to a growing and maturing believer, suffering is expected to be a daily part of their lives. Outside of Christendom, this sounds utterly ridiculous and not realistic.

Honestly, when thinking from a natural mind's point of view, it is easy to understand why many think suffering should not be a part of this walk.

Actually, I can recall as a younger pastors teaching falsely that all I had to do was become a Christian, and "everything would be all right."

This erroneous teaching could not have been further from the truth. As I would find out as I became older, this was not true.

Let's see what the *Scriptures* say about suffering.

> "These things I have spoken unto you, that in me ye might have peace. In the world ye shall have tribulation: but be of good cheer; I have overcome the world" (John 16:33, KJV).

Beloved, I pose a question to you, are we better than Jesus? To make it plain, Jesus suffered throughout his entire thirty-three years on earth. Are we better than he?

The epistles of *Matthew, Mark, Luke,* and *John* are written to expose Jesus's constant torment by the status quo of that day.

Every human being born after Adam and Eve were born with a propensity to sin naturally. I know this is not what is being taught in many congregations, but this is the truth. Our sin has caused suffering in the world. Yes, this assessment is directed to every human who was born after *the fall* in Genesis, including you and me.

Regardless of what is being taught in churches, the public places, the higher learning institutions, or elsewhere, not one of us is innocent.

According to the *Scriptures*, *"For all have sinned, and come short of the glory of God"* (Rom. 3:23, KJV).

The *Scriptures* are clear and concise; we are all guilty. I realize this does not give you a warm and fuzzy feeling, but it is the truth, and it is biblically sound.

In Genesis 3, sin entered into the world through one man, Adam; therefore, sin and suffering is what we all endure.

> *"Wherefore, as by one man sin entered into the world, and death by sin; and so death passed upon all men, for that all have sinned" (Rom. 5:12, KJV).*

Even though I am a born-again Christian, I still have a bent toward sin. My initial reaction, regardless of the circumstances, is to have my own way—just as you do.

I am always on guard with self-evaluation to ensure I do not offend *our Creator*. I naturally desire to have my way with things. It is as simple as exaggerating or telling a little white lie. I am not of this world, but I am still in this world, which means I will battle with sin until *the Rapture*. This is just the raw truth!

If anyone ever tells you they have overcome sin, please run from this person because this is simply not true!

Please read the *scripture* below:

> *"If we say that we have no sin, we deceive ourselves, and the truth is not in us"* (1 John 1:8, KJV).

Actually, truth be told, sinning is the most natural thing for me or any believer to do first.

Why is it a young baby or child never has to be taught to do wrong?

Why do I constantly struggle with my sin nature?

It is simple. All babies are born with a natural slant to sin, and this only get worse as time goes forward.

I know the above biblical assessment is not what you were taught early on. However, according to *Scriptures*, not one of us is born innocent.

> *"Behold, I was shapen in iniquity; and in sin did my mother conceive me"* (Ps. 51:5, KJV).

So are babies really born innocent as the masses would have you believe? Reality is this, as long as you and I are on this earth, we will struggle with sin.

You see, before you and I became born-again Christians, we did as we please. We did not consider whether our choices were right or wrong.

Honestly, you and I did not care whether our choices were offensive to *our Creator* or anyone else. I can only speak for myself here, but I lived at will, and I did what I wanted to do. I pleased the flesh. Of course, I reaped the benefits of living at will too.

The chaos within my life was proof positive that living as I pleased was not working very well. I lived this way for many years before I was humbled to change.

Can you identify with my previous lifestyle above?

Do you think I should have surrendered earlier?

I realize these questions are redundant, but I put the questions forth to cause you to think. It is absolutely ridiculous (looking back) how many years I wasted due to my chosen rebellious lifestyle.

I am so thankful to *the Father* that I did not die in my sin. I could have left this earth in the lost state I was in, as so many others have done. I give *Him* complete honor and glory for saving me from myself, until this day.

> *"For when we were yet without strength, in due time Christ died for the ungodly.*
>
> *"For scarcely for a righteous man will one die: yet peradventure for a good man some would even dare to die.*
>
> *"But God commendeth his love toward us, in that, while we were yet sinners, Christ died for us.*
>
> *"Much more then, being now justified by his blood, we shall be saved from wrath through him.*
>
> *"For if, when we were enemies, we were reconciled to God by the death of his Son, much more, being reconciled, we shall be saved by his life.*
>
> *"And not only so, but we also joy in God through our Lord Jesus Christ, by whom we have now received the atonement"* (Rom. 5:6–11, KJV).

Jesus had mercy on my soul and gave me unmerited grace, which I did not deserve. Let me be clear, I still do not deserve *His* grace and mercy, and neither do you, beloved.

It was and still is because of *the Father's* goodness and unexplainable love for us that *He* extends *His* free gift of salvation.

According to the *scripture* listed above, Romans 5:10, we were once *His* enemies. Can you believe that? Just imagine, all born-again believers were previously an enemy to the *Creator of the universe*! *God* sent *His* only begotten son, *Jesus Christ*, to atone for and to be a living sacrifice for our past, present, and future sins.

> *"For God so loved the world, that He gave His only begotten Son, that whoever believes in Him shall not perish, but have eternal life"* (John 3:16, NASB).

Think about the sacrifices *He* made for us! They were huge!

Have you seen the movie made several years ago directed by Mel Gibson? *The Passion of the Christ?*

The movie was extremely difficult to watch without weeping throughout the entire three hours. The *Scriptures* became undeniably real on the big screen.

After watching *The Passion of the Christ*, I felt even more guilty and convicted of my sins. If Jesus's suffering for me was anything close to what was depicted in this movie, I cannot see how anyone can see this movie and not be humbled to change.

I began to see how when I choose *to do things my way* or *to have my own way*, how I nail Christ back on the cross over and over again.

By choosing sin, basically I am saying, "Christ you died for nothing."

Allow me to make this personal. When you choose sin over obedience to *the Word*, you are nailing *Him* back on the cross too (*figuratively speaking*).

I realize most believers do not think in these terms, but this is how we should think. No, this assessment is not in the Bible. This is purely my human analogy. Surely, the picture I have painted for you thus far has begun to resonate in your mind.

I wrote this book with you in mind.

There are so many critical biblical teachings within the *body of Christ* that are not being taught for many reasons. I am not sure exactly what is causing this problem within congregations, except I can recall what I experienced in past churches I attended. I suspect there are many false teachers and unqualified people teaching the Bible.

Sadly, it has been my experience in the past that Sunday school-teachers, Bible study teachers, and even pastors have not been called by God to teach the *Word of God*.

As shocking as this is to you, it is true all across our great nation. So many of these folks are teaching in complete error, not to mention grieving the *Holy Spirit*.

Teachers, evangelists, pastors, or orators of the *Holy Scriptures* must be called by God to teach the Bible. Let's see what the *Scriptures* say about this touchy subject matter.

> *"Show yourself in all respects to be a model of good works, and in your teaching show integrity, dignity, and sound speech that cannot be condemned, so that an opponent may be put to shame, having nothing evil to say about us"* (Titus 2:7–8, ESV).

You see, teaching *Scriptures* are a gift from God. *The Father* will engage the *Holy Spirit* to teach those *He* has called to teach, so those called will be qualified to teach.

> *"Study to shew thyself approved unto God, a workman that needeth not to be ashamed, rightly dividing the word of truth"* (2 Tim. 2:15, KJV).

> *"Therefore whoever relaxes one of the least of these commandments and teaches others to do the same will be called least in the kingdom of heaven, but whoever does them and teaches them will be called great in the kingdom of heaven"* (Matt. 5:19, ESV).

> *"Desiring to be teachers of the law, without understanding either what they are saying or the things about which they make confident assertions. Now we know that the law is good, if one uses it lawfully"* (1 Tim. 1:7–8).

> *"Having gifts that differ according to the grace given to us, let us use them: if prophecy, in proportion to our faith; if service, in our serving; the one who teaches, in his teaching"* (Rom. 12:6, ESV).

All *scriptures* were inspired by God, Himself!

> *"All scripture is breathed out by God and profitable for teaching, for reproof, for correction, and for training in righteousness"* (2 Tim. 3:16, ESV).

"But the Comforter, which is the Holy Ghost, whom the Father will send in my name, he shall teach you all things, and bring all things to your remembrance, whatsoever I have said unto you" (John 14:26, KJV).

"But when the Comforter is come, whom I will send unto you from the Father, even the Spirit of truth, which proceedeth from the Father, he shall testify of me" (John 15:26, KJV).

This is why, *"My brethren, be not many masters, knowing that we shall receive the greater condemnation"* (James 3:1, KJV).

Teaching the *Scriptures* is very serious business regardless of how congregations or pastors attempt to minimize it.

Did you know if a person is teaching *the Word* in error, there will be biblical consequences? James 3:1, listed above, it does not say what the consequences will be, but I totally believe what it states.

After studying and considering the above *scriptures*, do you believe *the Creator* approves just anyone teaching the Bible?

Pastors who permit people who have not been called by God to teach the *Scriptures*, to rightly divide the Word of truth, will be held accountable.

I cannot tell you how many times over the last thirty-plus years I have observed public school teachers being appointed to teach Sunday school because they were a schoolteacher. Or it could also be that an individual was a friend of the pastors or his wife and the person contributed a lot of "good works" to the congregation. The list goes on and on with regard to unqualified people teaching the *Scriptures*.

I submit to you today, this is still happening within many churches.

Please know if any *body of Christ* operates in biblical error or teachings, this congregation will be dysfunctional, at best.

Please take time to study *New Testament* books of Romans, Corinthians, Galatians, Ephesians, Colossians, 1 Timothy, Philippians, etc.

I make this suggestion because you will see how many of the early churches were operating in error too. Paul wrote letters to the churches above to point out biblical error and correction (1 Tim.).

Who within congregations are biblically astute enough to point out biblical error in the twenty-first century?

There have been many times when I have been in church service, and the pastor was turning to *Scripture* reading, and he told the congregation they did not have to open their Bibles. What! Of course, many of the parishioners obeyed the pastor's erroneous command. I named just a few major faults within the *body of Christ* regarding teaching the Bible.

And the faults I have named are major because these errors are causing believers to stumble and even fail.

There is another major issue that I will address. Many believers do not study the Bible as the *Scriptures* commands.

Please know there are many other hindrances within congregations that contribute to the believers' spiritual growth. However, I decided to focus on the main two you are probably familiar with.

"Study to shew thyself approved unto God, a workman that needeth not to be ashamed, rightly dividing the word of truth" (2 Tim. 2:15, KJV).

Therefore, believers who do not study the Bible daily limit God's absolute power through the *Holy Spirit* to teach *His* ways and reveal biblical interpretation of *the Word*.

It is no wonder many believers within Christendom suffer from lack of knowledge regarding the true meaning of *Scriptures*.

Do you think my assessment has merit? How can you know you are being taught in biblical error if you do not study and apply the *Scriptures* yourself?

Many believers trust and follow their pastors and other leadership figures within the church because they do not study for themselves.

You see, Jesus never suggested to us in the *Scriptures* to follow any man.

Jesus said, "Follow me."

> *"Then Jesus said to his disciples, "Whoever wants to be my disciple must deny themselves and take up their cross and follow me" (Matt. 6:24, KJV).*

There are many other *scriptures* listed within the *New Testament* where Jesus reiterated who you are to follow.

Beloved, I am not suggesting to you not to listen to your pastor or Bible teachers if they are following Jesus's examples. The only way you will know this is if you have spent quality time studying and allowing the *Holy Spirit* to plant *God's* word on your heart. And the *Holy Spirit* will take up residence within your heart to supply you with the gift of discernment and other spiritual gifts.

The gift of discernment will reveal all manner of biblical error (i.e., false prophets, erroneous Bible teachings, people who are masquerading as believers, and many other unnamed errors).

It is a natural progression; when believers do not study the Bible for themselves, by default, they live in error for years.

In other words, believers do not live the life *God* intended for them, largely due to ignorance of what *His* Word commands.

> *"My people are destroyed for lack of knowledge: because thou hast rejected knowledge, I will also reject thee, that thou shalt be no priest to me: seeing thou hast forgotten the law of thy God, I will also forget thy children" (Hosea 4:6, KJV).*

To interpret, it will be impossible for you to think your *suffering was worth it* if you are living the Christian life in error or through your powerless efforts.

Basically, you cannot have a biblical revelation or understanding of suffering when you do not know the full range of understanding what Jesus went through for you.

I make this statement because if the aforementioned assessment describes where you're at in your walk, you are walking without power and in your human wisdom.

The biblical term for this is called *carnal minded*, as addressed in chapter 6. Therefore, you are walking out the Christian life in your own strength, without *God's* help. This is not good by any stretch of the imagination. You are missing out on *God's* amazing grace and *His* best for you.

Beloved, I hope this chapter has shed light on where you are in your walk with Christ.

Here are some questions to prompt deep thought:

1. Do you study the Bible daily with intent to allow the *Holy Spirit* to teach you?
2. Do you apply or integrate the *Scriptures'* teachings into your life immediately?
3. Are you a member within a congregation where biblical error is embraced? If so, leave immediately.
4. Are you committed to biblical and spiritual growth?

These are only a few questions that will be helpful in moving you toward maturity as a Christian in *The Word* for your growth.

CHAPTER 10

Spread the Word

"In your Law it is written that the testimony of two people is true. I am the one who bears witness about myself, and the Father who sent me bears witness about me" (John 8:17–18, ESV).

When you are blessed to receive divine revelation regarding your *"hope deferred state,"* please share your experiences with others.

If *our Father* has not revealed why *hope is deferred* but still you have chosen to be obedient, sharing your story of obedience will give glory to *our Father* in heaven. Plus, others will be encouraged beyond what you could ever imagine. Believers need to be encouraged by other believer's triumphs.

"Therefore encourage one another and build up one another, just as you also are doing" (1 Thess. 5:11, NASB).

Please know that encouraging other believers within the *body of Christ* will help with their spiritual growth process. The truth of the matter is, someone in our lives stopped by to encourage each one of us along this spiritual journey. We should all desire to see other believers grow in real biblical understanding and growth. There may be various reasons preventing you from sharing *His* divine revelations. For instance, some believers are paralyzed by fear because they are not sure how to go about spreading the Word.

First thing to consider is, "For God hath not given us the spirit of fear; but of power, and of love, and of a sound mind" (2 Tim. 1:7, KJV).

Plus, some within the *body of Christ* are afraid because they are not sure what to say or how to say it. Remember, this is what *our Father* did for Moses within the Old Testament. According to the *Scriptures*, Moses was concerned about his inability to speak eloquently.

> *"And Moses said unto the LORD, O my Lord, I am not eloquent, neither heretofore, nor since thou hast spoken unto thy servant: but I am slow of speech, and of a slow tongue" (Exod. 4:10, KJV).*

If you completely trust *our Creator*, it will not be necessary to be concerned about what to say. Humble yourself and ask *Him* to help you.

> *"And the LORD said unto him, Who hath made man's mouth? or who maketh the dumb, or deaf, or the seeing, or the blind? have not I the LORD? Now therefore go, and I will be with thy mouth, and teach thee what thou shalt say" (Exod. 4:11–12, KJV).*

Our Father will do for you what *He* did for Moses. I am speaking from the standpoint of experience because *He* did it for me.

Also, you may be discouraged due to jealousy from other carnal-minded Christians, so be careful with who you share what *He* is doing for you and through you.

I experienced members in congregations with unbelievable jealousy covered under the disguise of concern or desiring to help me.

Not everyone will be happy for you. As a matter of fact, many will be jealous but will attempt to hide it. If you are discerning, the *Holy Spirit* will reveal these folks to you.

As I humbled myself to Bible teachings daily and permitted the *Holy Spirit* would take over my psyche, I began to see things from God's point of view. It is better to navigate your thoughts toward what the *Scripture* says rather than your own.

> *"For the Holy Ghost shall teach you in the same hour what ye ought to say" (Luke 12:12 KJV).*

The more I adhered to the promptings of the *Holy Spirit* to *"share my story"* or to *"spread the Word,"* the more confidence *He* gave me. We all have a story to tell of failure, suffering, trials and tribulations, loss, bad decisions, and the list is goes on. Sure, you can reside in the universe of your choosing, but *He* will hold you accountable.

Remember this verse:

> *"But he that knew not, and did commit things worthy of stripes, shall be beaten with few stripes. For unto whomsoever much is given, of him shall be much required: and to whom men have committed much, of him they will ask the more" (Luke 12:48, KJV).*

If you have not determined yet, all your personal trials and sufferings were part of a divine plan to grow you spiritually and biblically.

I am not sure what you have been taught up until this point regarding your role as a born-again believer. *The Father* has worked through me to give great insight on what your role should be going forward. You see, we were all created to serve *our Creator* and to give *Him* glory with our lives. *He* never intended for us *to do our own thing*.

> *"Blessed be the God and Father of our Lord Jesus Christ, who has blessed us with every spiritual blessing in the heavenly places in Christ, just as He chose us in Him before the foundation of the world that*

we should be holy and blameless before Him. In love He predestined us to adoption as sons through Christ Jesus to Himself, according to the good pleasure of His will, to the praise of the glory of His grace... In Him we have obtained an inheritance, having been predestined according to His purpose who works all things after the counsel of His will" (Eph. 1:2–5, 11 KJV).

Beloved, keep in mind, *the Father* will not send you to witness for *Him* without equipping you. If you trust *Him*, it is impossible for *Him* to fail you.

"But my God shall supply all your need according to his riches in glory by Christ Jesus.

Now unto God and our Father be glory for ever and ever. Amen" (Phil. 4:19–20, KJV).

As a follower of *Jesus Christ*, there will always be times of *deferred hope*. It took me many, many years to understand.

Just imagine, if everything went our way, there would not be a need to humble ourselves and submit to a *Holy God*.

Everything would revolve around the "universe of me," which would not be a good thing.

Now many have chosen to be on their thrones, and it has been costly.

Where would God get the glory in my ridiculous, nonsensical way of living? Again, I know this sounds comical, but many within the *body of Christ* have chosen this path.

Anyone who calls themselves a Christian must submit to *the Creator's* absolute sovereign rule and authority over and in their lives. However, this is what many believers do not do.

If the believer does not surrender his or her will to *His* divine direction and authority, there will be chaos. This person will be a distorted picture of Christianity.

Also, this person will see themselves as righteous in their own eyes. However, this is a person who has chosen self-deception at all cost.

> *"There is a generation that are pure in their own eyes, and yet are not washed from their filthiness" (Prov. 30:12, KJV).*

> *"Every way of a man is right in his own eyes: but the LORD pondereth the hearts" (Prov. 21:2, KJV).*

I have been very careful to list throughout this book a litany of benefits of why submitting your complete will to *His* will is beneficial. And I have carefully listed the fallout of not adhering to stern biblical warnings, not to mention, I have learned from direct experience of the years of delayed blessings I caused.

Let me park here for a moment, blessings will not be as the world considers blessings. The blessings the world and some churches will have you to believe waiting for you is status, financial wealth, title, or "name it and claim it." The list goes on.

To interpret clearly, if your ways are pleasing to God, the blessings received will be spiritual and biblical knowledge growth, which will include but are not limited to the gifts of the Spirit.

> *"Now concerning spiritual gifts, brethren, I would not have you ignorant.*
>
> *Ye know that ye were Gentiles, carried away unto these dumb idols, even as ye were led.*
>
> *Wherefore I give you to understand, that no man speaking by the Spirit of God calleth Jesus accursed: and that no man can say that Jesus is the Lord, but by the Holy Ghost.*
>
> *Now there are diversities of gifts, but the same Spirit.*
>
> *And there are differences of administrations, but the same Lord.*

And there are diversities of operations, but it is the same God which worketh all in all.

But the manifestation of the Spirit is given to every man to profit withal.

For to one is given by the Spirit the word of wisdom; to another the word of knowledge by the same Spirit;

To another faith by the same Spirit; to another the gifts of healing by the same Spirit;

To another the working of miracles; to another prophecy; to another discerning of spirits; to another divers kinds of tongues; to another the interpretation of tongues:

But all these worketh that one and the selfsame Spirit, dividing to every man severally as he will" (1 Cor. 12, KJV).

Beloved, what I am saying is that *the Father* will empower you to spread the gospel beyond your human limitations. *He* will bless you with some or all the gifts listed above (as *He* chooses) to further the gospel.

I am not saying *He* will not bless you financially or materially; I am just saying a financial blessing is not the priority. *God* is not part of the "let's make a deal" crowd, nor is *He* into the "name and claim it" crowd.

Furthering the gospel or fulfilling *the Great Commission* (Matt. 28:18–20) is paramount to *Him*.

As *God* equipped the saints of old within the Old and New Testaments, *He* will equip you to be a powerful force for the cause of Christ if you trust *Him*.

Beloved, there are two things at stake here: lost souls and *His* glory.

The Father desires to engage you to action for *His* divine cause.

As the modern day, twenty-first century church moves toward confusion, embracing sinful teachings and false doctrines, immorality of every kind, rejection of absolute biblical truth, and entertainment, God still cares about *His* glory!

Contrary to what is being taught in some congregations, according to the *Scriptures*, *He* will not trade, nor will *He* sacrifice *His* sovereignty or glory to please man.

> *"I am the LORD: that is my name: and my glory will I not give to another, neither my praise to graven images"* (Isa. 42:8, KJV).

> *"For my own sake, for my own sake, I do this. How can I let myself be defamed? I will not yield my glory to another"* (Isa. 48:11, KJV).

I plugged in *scriptures* within each chapter because I have no desire for you to take my word (*I am flesh with human limitations*).

These *scriptures* confirm biblical validation of all comments I have brought forth within the pages of this book. On another front, many congregations seem to lack zeal or a since of urgency when it comes to carrying out *the Great Commission*.

Every mature believer should be compelled by direction of the *Holy Spirit* to use their *"deferred hope status"* as a call to serve.

The truth is, as a follower of *Jesus Christ*, there will always be opposition, disappointments, rejection, deferred hope, lack of funds, and contentious people to deal with, to name a few. Are you going to continue to permit life issues to be an excuse not to be obedient?

You see, someone within your sphere of influence needs to actually see a believer who is walking what they talk. All too often, this is not the case.

Many times over, believers forfeit opportunities of being real witnesses because they become so overwhelmed with the cares of this world.

> *"And the cares of this world, and the deceitfulness of riches, and the lusts of other things entering in, choke the word, and it becometh unfruitful"* (Mark 4:19).

Simply stated, it is because many believe their problems should govern their lives. This could not be further from the truth. Much of your weariness results from your constant battle against these components. However, you are on the path of *His* choosing, so do not give up! Hope in *Him*, for you will again praise *Him* for the help of *His* presence.

I have come to realize one main point about this life: all of what you are going through is temporary. It is of no consequence if it does not feel like your troubles are temporary or whether or not you believe it. Your circumstances are temporary, according to the *Scriptures*.

> *"And God shall wipe away all tears from their eyes; and there shall be no more death, neither sorrow, nor crying, neither shall there be any more pain: for the former things are passed away"* (Rev. 21:4).

It is true; all of us have to go about our daily business of working a job and taking care of our families and all this entails.

But as believers, there is more to attending Bible study, attending church, and singing in the choir, being a deacon or deaconess, teaching Bible classes, being an usher, or being a pastor or a church member.

All the above church functions or roles are related to administration within the *body of Christ*, which does have a place, but none of the above-listed items are more important than studying the Bible and reaching out to lost souls.

Whatever capacity you are serving in with the body, be careful not to become consumed by your role.

I have attended many congregations in the past where the congregation was totally caught up in the ushers' annual day or pastors' annual day or church annual day (*none of this is in the Bible*), and every year this would be the focus.

Do you think *the Father* honored man's traditions?

> *"Beware lest any man spoil you through philosophy and vain deceit, after the tradition of men, after the rudiments of the world, and not after Christ"* (Col. 2:8, KJV).

Please know the members of these congregations were very sincere in carrying out their tasks, but the traditions should not have been the focal point throughout the year.

Can you imagine how many potential souls that could have been saved?

All too often, many congregations are consumed with traditions or tasks that have no eternal value. Actually many of these rituals borders on human worship by default.

To interpret, congregations that practice such traditions must be careful, and I say *congregations* because congregations are supposed to represent *the church* or *the Bride of Christ*. When congregations practice men's traditions, they are representative of the world.

This is called sin, plain and simple.

Beloved, *the Father* does not honor sin of any kind regardless of how long someone has been in church, their pedigree, their relatives or ancestors, or who their affiliations are with. I know you have been associated with people who love to tell you about their mothers and fathers or other relatives who have been in the church for years and years. Some love to tell you they are a deacon, pastor, usher, in the choir or other service or how religious they are, not realizing these very admissions testifies against them.

The only thing I should be bragging about is Christ and only Christ.

Paul said it best when he said, "But may it never be that I would boast, except in the cross of our Lord Jesus Christ, through which the world has been crucified to me, and I to the world" (Gal. 6:14, KJV).

There is no such thing of people as being declared righteous due to affiliation or association with a certain person or group of people.

I have been surprised and completely caught off guard when I ask someone if they have been saved through *Jesus Christ*. The answers I have received over the years have been nothing short of shocking.

Some would say that they were a member of such and such church and so and so was their pastor. What? Of course, as the *Holy Spirit* guided me to do so, I would teach some the truth, and I say *some* because the *Holy Spirit* does not always permit me to witness to everyone.

According to the *Scriptures*, the only person ever declared righteous was Abraham in the *Old Testament*.

> *"For if Abraham were justified by works, he hath whereof to glory; but not before God. For what saith the scripture? Abraham believed God, and it was counted unto him for righteousness. Now to him that worketh is the reward not reckoned of grace, but of debt"* (Rom. 4:2–4, KJV).

According to what the *New Testament* verses say, we must accept *Jesus Christ* as our personal savior, or *we must be born* again, and this is the only way to be justified in the sight of *God*.

Jesus told Nicodemus in the book of John, "Jesus answered and said unto him, Verily, verily, I say unto thee, Except a man be born again, he cannot see the kingdom of God" (John 3:3, KJV).

> *"Marvel not that I said unto thee, Ye must be born again"* (John 3:7, KJV).

Beloved, the hope we have is not of this world, so is your hope really deferred?

Looking back on my life, I believe everything that happened in my world was orchestrated by divine providence to give *the Father* glory. Sure, I made terrible choices, and *He* permitted the chaos to continue until I humbled myself completely as *His* servant.

You see, there is your plan, and then there is *His* plan. Which plan carries the most weight?

As born-again believers in anticipation of our coming King, the Lamb of God's return, we eagerly await the rapture of *His* bride (the church, which is us).

"Let us be glad and rejoice, and give honour to him: for the marriage of the Lamb is come, and his wife hath made herself ready. And to her was granted that she should be arrayed in fine linen, clean and white: for the fine linen is the righteousness of saints. And he saith unto me, Write, Blessed [are] they which are called unto the marriage supper of the Lamb. And he saith unto me, These are the true sayings of God" (Rev. 19:7–9).

"Husbands, love your wives, even as Christ also loved the church, and gave himself for it;

That he might sanctify and cleanse it with the washing of water by the word,

That he might present it to himself a glorious church, not having spot, or wrinkle, or any such thing; but that it should be holy and without blemish" (Eph. 5).

This is why it is absolutely crucial that all congregations who claim to open in the name of *Jesus Christ* must represent *the church,* or else they are in danger of representing the doctrines of men.

Christ will come to claim *the church* upon *His* return. Those *within the church* who are "actively teaching and living out *His* divine will" will be ready (1 Thess. 4:16–17, NASB).

Please do not misunderstand, some traditions are good to edify the *body of Christ,* but many traditions are a hindrance, at best.

Hopefully, you are headed in the right direction and this book has opened your mind to new possibilities.

If one moves away from living and practicing biblical error, this opens the door for God to enact real change. However, on the opposite end of this spectrum, living in biblical error knowingly (as many do) ties *the Creator's* hands making Him unable to assist them.

There are many ways one can be functioning in biblical error, but due to embraced self-deception, it becomes harder to identify for those who are practicing it.

I am prayerful and hopeful the above assessment no longer applies to you.

Beloved, my hope is you are no longer shrouded in doubt, misunderstandings, and incorrect biblical teachings or bound by satanic strongholds or devices at this point.

I pray that *the Father* has used me to reach into the depths of your soul for eternal change. I would suggest studying the Bible diligently. Utilize this book as reference tools in the future. My book should *never* take the place of *Scripture*.

Beloved, I make the above suggestions because how you proceed forward will have lasting effects on everyone in your sphere of influence and beyond, not to mention where you will spend all *eternity*.

Hopefully, you realize going forward in absolute truth and divinely inspired direction by the *Holy Spirit* will breathe life into your very existence.

You will never be the same!

ABOUT THE AUTHOR

My name is Tonya R. Williams.

She enjoys writing Christian books to inspire the earth's inhabitants, reading books, going to the movies, traveling, staying in-tune with national and international events and exercising.

She is the Mom of four sons: Anthony, Eddie, Derek and Vincent, Jr. She's been married to her husband, Vincent for 25 years. She is a sister to five brothers and two sisters. She is a grandmother of five grandchildren. In her free time, she loves traveling nationally and internationally and writing in her spare time.

Her current book, "What To Do When Hope is Deferred" was written to encourage and enlighten new believer's, middle of the road believers and seasoned believers to forge an understanding of their deferred hope status. All while sharing with her readers how to live their lives to give God glory.

She carefully laid out particular reasons why you're "hope is deferred" and what a believer is to do while being tried in the fire.

Her lovingly inspired and provoked readers to mentally transform to no longer live in mediocrity and to change their mindsets with the intent to influence others to live out real Christianity.

She believes her universal message of love for God, service to others and Bible studying has compelled her to write powerful books that teach uncompromising truth.

She challenges every reader to live with intent to apply biblical absolutes - void of hypocrisy.

In the years ahead, Tonya looks forward to writing more books. All while making a positive impact on the world and influencing souls to be saved and minds to yield toward Our Creator.

CPSIA information can be obtained
at www.ICGtesting.com
Printed in the USA
FFHW022119250919
55215243-60939FF